Grow Up!

No, Really.

Grow Up!

No, Really.

Matthew Harms

To everyone who continues to support me in doing what I was always told could never be done, I appreciate your support more than words can ever express.

I may not be perfect but you help me overlook the shortcomings and focus on the strengths. Those who cannot do, teach. I still find that ironic and inspirational.

Other Books by Matthew Harms:

Employed! A Career Readiness Manual

As a bonus for anyone buying this book...

Visit www.matthewbharms.com and go to the "Bonus Content" link from the main menu. Then select "Grow Up" and enter Adulting2020 for the password. This will entitle you to a free downloadable PDF of all the worksheets that were included at the back of each chapter. You can print them and complete by hand or click and fill so that you always have a digital copy. You can also reach out through the site with any questions, concerns, feedback or success stories that you would like to share.

Table of Contents:

INTRODUCTION

Have you ever thought that by finishing school, getting a high school diploma – possibly even becoming an overachiever and going on to college, you would have all of the knowledge you need to strike out on your own? Maybe you received some of the same advice in those crucial teenage years that I did when I allowed the outside world, close friends and family included in that broad generalization, to convince me that college was an absolute necessity. No, this book is not going to bash education, but if that is what you are hoping for, please keep reading and I doubt you will be disappointed.

While I graduated from college over a decade ago, I recently began working in a coaching and teaching capacity with our city's youth – ranging from eleven to eighteen years in age. Less than a week in, and the experience had already confirmed for me that nothing has changed in all these years. For all the technological, medical and other advancements our society has made, there is still one painful fact that has remained the same. Our education system does not teach what our youth need to learn in order to become self-sufficient contributing members of society. Expensive, high profile schools are no exception to this phenomenon either; you may learn how to calculate the square root of 81 ($\sqrt{81}$) by using apples and oranges, but can you balance a checking account? Can you become a resident expert at philosophy and world religions? Absolutely. How about understanding the basics of how credit card interest rates work? Not so much!

Book smart and brain dead; that expression sums up the issue in a nutshell. And because this problem has gone unaddressed for so long, the vicious cycle is perpetuated from generation to generation. I am about ten years older than many of my friends, acquaintances, and coworkers, and some of the questions and comments I hear about real-world situations are downright frightening. Since we are not properly educating folks when they are in school, they wind up becoming the next generation of parents who have muddled through some of these decisions and challenges. And, through no fault of their own, try to provide guidance and advice based on the way they learn to do things and not necessarily on the facts and figures behind those recommendations.

I make no claims at being an expert in any of the areas that will be mentioned in this book, but I do have enough knowledge and hands-on experience with them to raise some important questions many others would prefer to leave unspoken. The goal is not to make you a master at what has commonly been dubbed "adulting" by those fresh out of school or moving out of their parents' basement, but rather to shine light on the things all of us may not know and society takes for granted. Some of the topics mentioned are ones I was fortunate enough to learn about through an extensive career working in the banking and finance industry where I was able to leverage from the mistakes of others as well as the on the job training that was provided. Other topics were learned the same way I do anytime I don't understand something – by voraciously reading about it through books, the Internet, magazines, and newspapers.

At the end of each chapter in this book I have included different activity or worksheets to help you organize your thoughts or practice your skills. Feel free to write right on the page or transfer them to a notebook or journal if that works better for you. They are also available in downloadable PDF format from my website if a digital solution is easier to work with. There is no right of wrong way to use the sheets so long as you are using them so way! I cannot stress enough the importance of research and reflection in supporting your personal growth.

So without any further ado, let's dive right in!

"Compound interest is the eighth wonder of the world. He who understands it, earns it…he who doesn't…pays."

-Albert Einstein

Chapter 1: Interest Rates

I know, I know. Most introductory level economics or finance classes discuss interest rates, right? Why then would anyone start a book with a topic that contradicts my claim about school not teaching us about the real world? The answer to both of those questions has everything to do with the difference between book smarts and the real-world application of those principles. Were you taught how an interest rate can affect virtually every aspect of your life, or strictly what it is and maybe how to calculate it? No need to answer; I've worked with enough people to know that the vast majority can provide a textbook definition at best and starry-eyed gaze at worst.

Interest rates can work both for and against you in life. When you are being "charged" interest, it is advantageous to negotiate the lowest possible rate so that you are paying the least amount of money unnecessarily. That seems to be a concept more people understand than the opposite, which is when you are earning interest, it is in your *best interest* to have as high a rate as possible. While this is not meant to be an economics book, what I will say is that the rates at any given point in time will always be higher for borrowing than what you will earn. The reason for that is that banking is a big business. These institutions pay you one rate to keep your money on deposit with them, then turn around and lend it out at higher rates. How do you think they afford all of those big beautiful buildings?

We cannot control how high or low interest rates are in general, that is the job of the Federal Reserve (the Fed), and the banks in turn use these guidelines to set their rates and compete for your business. What we can control is how much research we put into the different options before making a long-term commitment. There are so many resources out there to help guide you in the right direction that there is no excuse for being uninformed. Some of my favorite sites when in need of a quick reference are:

➢ Nerdwallet.com
➢ Lendingtree.com
➢ Bankrate.com

Paying Interest

Unless you are living off the grid or are so incredibly wealthy that you have no need for borrowing money, interest rates are going to directly control how much of your paycheck you get to keep every month. If you have a credit card that is not paid in full by the due date, you are feeling the effect of interest rates. Want to go a step further? How much you pay for your monthly car payment –

if you are financing instead of leasing – is directly related to your interest rate. And the biggest purchase, as well as monthly payment you are bound to encounter, is on your mortgage. For those still at the very onset of becoming an adult, a mortgage is basically just a big loan the bank provides to help with the purchase of a home. But have no fear; this will be discussed in more detail later on along with the main factors that determine your interest rate – credit scores.

So, let's talk about credit cards. Full disclosure, I have more than I can count and am a huge proponent of the benefits they afford modern society – when used responsibly. You can effectively buy things now and pay for them later, earn cashback rewards for every dollar you spend (if you're not earning anything – switch cards now) and are provided far more security and consumer protections than paying by cash or debit cards. For those who are responsible, and understand the intricacies of paying bills on time and inspecting spending history for accuracy, credit cards are indispensable.

For those who struggle keeping their pet rock alive, and remembering to pay your bills falls into that same category, credit cards can set you up for failure and ruin years of your life. At the time of writing this, the average credit card interest rate in the United States is just under 20%. If that number doesn't seem high enough as it is, remember that this is not the highest rate you may encounter and the less qualified you are to borrow money the higher that rate will be. Rates of 30% and higher are not uncommon, and some issuers have made publicity for charging rates of almost 80% when cardholders become delinquent on payments.

Let's think about that in terms of dollars and cents for a moment. Imagine you borrowed $1,000 at 20%. The interest cost of that becomes $200 for the year, or $17 a month. The same $1,000 at 80% is $800 a year in interest, or $67 a month. The minimum payment the credit card company requires is generally only slightly higher than your monthly interest charge, which is specifically designed to keep you in debt to them forever. If your monthly interest is $17 and the minimum payment is $20, it means that only $3 every month is paying back your original $1,000 balance. At that rate, it will take approximately 330 months to pay back the loan. That's a whopping 27 years!

Within the credit card family are the "no interest" financing gimmicks that you can encounter in any number of forms, most commonly in the department store when you get to the checkout counter. The cashier will let you know that you can buy everything in your shopping cart without paying for it today by applying for one of their credit cards. If you get approved, there is generally a fixed period of time where you can pay the purchase off without incurring any interest charge. Sounds like a great deal, right?

There are a few reasons you should be wary of this *gift* the store is trying to bestow on you. The first is directly related to what happens if you miss a payment or do not pay the balance off in full by the expiration date. In these instances you can forfeit that 0% interest rate and now find yourself responsible for all of the interest accrued since day one. The second reason is one that will come up again later in the book, but you want to be wary about having too many credit accounts, and store-specific cards provide you the least ongoing benefit after that initial promotion expires.

In comparison to credit cards, the interest rates on car loans can appear to be much more attractive. But that is the illusion car dealerships and finance companies want you to believe. In certain parts of the country, driving is a necessity for adults. With a lack of adequate infrastructure such as mass transportation, taxis, rideshares and the like, owning a car becomes the only way to get to work or take the kids to school. The auto industry knows what a convenience it is to own your own vehicle and their seemingly altruistic advertisements of offering financing to everyone, no matter the income or credit situation, is a clever gimmick to lure you into believing your best intentions are the basis for this generosity. While credit cards do not have a legally imposed cap (maximum) on the interest rate, some states do protect consumers on car loans. But not all do, and for some that do have caps, they can still reach as high as 21%.

Unfortunately for a consumer, this is not where the bad news about auto loan rates ends. Unlike credit cards that are commonly unsecured debt, meaning it is very difficult for the lender to come after you for personal property if you do not pay; the car you are driving secures your auto loan. That basically means that you do not actually "own" the vehicle you are driving until you pay that loan back in full. That's right, the bank owns it and allows you to operate it. If you miss one or two credit card payments, you will incur some fees and possibly receive some nasty letters and phone calls, and lower your credit score. But miss one or two car payments and you may wake up to find that your vehicle has been repossessed.

Repossession is when the bank enlists a towing company to find your car and take it back without your permission – because they don't need to ask for it. At this point, you can just let them keep it and see how much money it will cost to settle up, or try and get it back. But in order to do the latter, not only are you going to need to pay back every dollar you owe the bank, but also the towing and impound fees – yep, those are not going to be waived because you finally decided to pay. In fact, you will most likely be responsible to pay these even if you let them keep the car!

The biggest pitfall in financing a car, outside of getting it repossessed, of course, is paying for it beyond its useful life. What does that mean? Basically, this – dealers love to sell customers on what the "monthly payment" will be. Let's be honest, most of us are conditioned to make a big purchase on whether or not it fits into our budget. But the real question we should be asking is, "What is the *total cost* of the financing?"

If you buy a ten-year-old car with a monthly payment you

can afford, but those payments are going to equate to you paying far more than what the car will be worth over the next seven years, what are you left with at the end? Hint, this is not a trick question. A seventeen-year-old car – that may, or may not still be functional – and way too much money spent. Oh, and the need to borrow more money to buy a new car and replace the one that is on its last legs.

There is one last creative way the dealerships try to make their offers seem more attractive – also commonly used by mortgage companies, but we will speak about that shortly – and that's known as a balloon payment. This is where they make that monthly payment as enticing as possible, then add all of the money you are not paying every month onto your last payment. So imagine paying $250 per month for 47 months on a 4-year loan. You're probably feeling pretty good that you are only $250 away from finally owning that car. Then, you open your final statement and see that your payoff amount is $2,650! How can that be possible?

Well, if the monthly payment should have been $300, but you insisted you could not afford that, how did the dealer magically save you $2,400 ($50/month x 48 months)? Was it at their own expense? In rare instances, maybe. The bulk of the time, nope, they buried it in the fine print. In this example, that final payment amount of $2,650 is the regularly scheduled payment of $250 plus the $2,400 they "saved" you along the way. Want to take a guess what happens if you are unable to make that final balloon payment? No one can say for sure, but one thing is certain, repossession is still a legal option for the bank. So, you paid almost four years on a car only to lose it due to deceptive financing and not being savvy enough to read all of the disclosures.

The last, and potentially most expensive piece of this section will talk about how interest rates on your mortgage can either help you own one of the biggest assets of your life or drain your bank account for the next ten to forty years. If you are interested in exactly how mortgages and home ownership work, you are in luck – that will be covered in another section. For now, I want to solely focus on the costs and potential pitfalls associated with this type of loan. We have already spoken at length about how a given interest rate and the amount you pay every month toward that loan will determine how long you may be paying the debt off. In the case of mortgages, like car loans, it is easy to get lulled into a false sense of security because you are told exactly how much you need to pay each month and for how long. No mysteries, right?

Not quite.

Let's start by looking at a very normal, typical mortgage scenario where there are no hidden catches or fine print. You buy a house for $250,000 (depending where you live in the country that number may seem high or low, but it's an easy number to work with) and leave the standard down payment of 20%, which means you are taking out a loan for $200,000. The bank offers you a 30-year mortgage at a 5% interest rate (which is about average in our current interest rate environment at the time of writing this). This means that your monthly payment will be around $1,075 for the next 360 months.

You make your payments diligently for the first fifteen years and assume that, because you are halfway through your loan, you should only owe about half of your original amount, right? This is where compound interest works against you. Since most of your payments in the first fifteen years are applied to interest and not principle, you will actually still owe approximately $130,000 instead of $100,000. The next shock associated with this same premise is how much you will have actually paid for that $200,000 mortgage over the course of thirty years. Because of the interest you are paying, the total amount of that loan is actually almost $390,000 – practically double the original loan! **(See Appendix 1-1)**

While the thirty-year mortgage is probably the most common – because it comes with the most manageable monthly payment – a fifteen-year term can save you far more than just fifteen years' worth of payments. Even though your monthly payment will be higher, it most certainly will not be double the thirty-year payment and will put a fortune of interest costs back into your pocket. For the same $200,000 loan, your monthly payment would be $1,582 and the total cost of the home would only be $284,685 – over $100,000 saved in interest!

This option does come with a huge word of caution, though. Once you pick a term, you cannot change your mind about it later. You will be stuck with it for the next fifteen years, unless you refinance the entire loan – which can be a costly process, as you will see later in the section on mortgages. This payment may seem manageable when you are young, single and lacking any other real monthly expenses. But, if five years down the road, you have kids in school, additional vehicles, or anything else that life throws at you, it becomes those new expenses that must be manipulated to fit into your new budget. (**See Appendix 1-2**)

If you now know that you don't like the idea of wasting all that money in interest over thirty years, but also do not want to commit to the higher payment of the fifteen-year mortgage, there is a very useful technique that can be employed to save you some of that interest expense while still retaining your flexibility. While the bank will give you a monthly payment amount, that is only the *minimum amount* you are required to pay and anything additional you send in will be automatically applied to the principal. So, with the payment of $1,075 per month, let's just say that you decide to round that off to an even $1,100. Simply adding an extra $25 to the monthly payment will save you nineteen months of payments, over a year and a half and $11,776 in interest alone over the life of the loan! (**See Appendix 1-3**)

Next, imagine if you made the fifteen-year payment for the first five years when you had the extra room in your budget to support it then went back to the $1,075 payment. For lack of an exact calculator to run this calculation, I am going to spread that extra $507 per month that you would have paid for 60 months

($30,420) over the entire life of the loan, or an acceleration of $85 per month. That would shave off fifty-five months, almost 5 years, and save you $33,100 in total interest! **(See Appendix 1-4)**

Now that we see how even a perfectly straightforward mortgage can have far-reaching financial consequences, it is time to switch to some of the creative ways that mortgage companies try to ensure you are comfortable enough with the monthly payment so that you agree to finance with them and they stand to profit from all of that interest money. The first is by using an adjustable-rate mortgage, commonly referred to as an ARM in the finance world. There should not be much of a surprise here considering the name gives away what is going on.

In this scenario, you'll be given a fixed interest rate for a specific period of time (generally 3, 5, 7 or 10 years, with 5 and 7 being the most popular options). After that fixed period of time is over, your interest rate now becomes *adjustable* every year on the anniversary of your loan date. So that 5% rate you had for the first five years and got comfortable with, can possibly jump to 7, 8, 9% or higher. There are some protections usually built-in to limit how much it can rise each year, and the maximum it can rise to over the life of the loan, but even this cannot stop that interest rate from potentially doubling or more by the time you reach the final payment.

The other trick that is not used as commonly as it was in the past, but still shows up from time to time, is that balloon payment we spoke about with auto loans. Imagine that you could not afford that $1,075 monthly payment, so the bank found a way to "help you out" and bring it in for $975, which was your maximum budget amount. That $100 per month you saved doesn't just vanish and must be paid at some point, along with all of the associated interest that has accumulated over thirty years, resulting in a balloon payment that could be in the area of $40,000.

Yep, that's more than most people's annual salary, and the bank will not always be willing to work with you if you cannot pay it. And just like in the car scenario, the bank still owns your house at this point. You have spent over $300,000 and now stand to have them foreclose (like repossession but of your home) over the remaining $40,000 balance. There is nothing fair or upstanding about this, but the only way to ensure it does not happen to you is to educate yourself and read everything carefully. If you don't understand something, ask!

Believe it or not, less than half the states require you to have a lawyer at real estate closings, which can be a good thing if you are experienced and do not want to incur the added expense. However, if this is your first time purchasing a home, and your state does not require one, it can lead to making a pennywise and pound-foolish mistake. Bottom line, if you live in a state that does not require an attorney, and finances and contracts are not your strong point, consider paying a little extra money upfront so they can break this all down for you and avoid a costly mistake down-the-line. **(See Appendix 1-5)**

Earning Interest

To understand just how impactful interest rates can be on your earning power, it is important to understand a concept known as "The Rule of 72." Despite the fact that this is a fairly simple theory, I managed to go through high school and college (where I majored in finance no less) without ever hearing it spoken of. I was in my twenties the first time an associate showed it to me on paper, and I was both skeptical and blown away at the same time. How could I spend all that money on a Bachelor's Degree without being taught this elementary school level theory? I won't answer that, but it is definitely instances like this that prompted me to write this book. The Rule of 72 basically states that if you take the number 72 and divide it by the interest rate you are earning on your money, the result will tell you how long it will take for your money to double.

Let's look at some examples:

@ 1%: 72 ÷ 1 = 72 years

@ 3%: 72 ÷ 3 = 24 years

@ 6%: 72 ÷ 6 = 12 years

@ 12% 72 ÷ 12 = 6 years

Grow Up!

If you were born in the last twenty-five years, you might be wondering where on Earth it is possible to get 12% interest. And honestly, that was a valid question even when I was younger and the best savings rates you could hope for were 2½% to 5%. But before I answer that, let's stress the importance of that Rule of 72. Let's say you put away $1,000 on your eighteenth birthday, the results would be as follows on your 90th birthday (and yes I know that sounds like a ridiculous age, but humor me for illustrative purposes):

$1,000 @ 1% = $2,000 @ 90 years old

$1,000 @ 3% = $8,000 @ 90 years old

$1,000 @ 6% = $64,000 @ 90 years old

$1,000 @ 12% = $4,096,000 @ 90 years old

How powerful is that? The same investment can either grow to $2,000 or over $4,000,000 without any extra work on your part, simply by seeking out the best interest rate and not touching the money. Really want to be mind blown? What would happen if you started with a $2,000 investment? That's right, everything doubles! And if you continue to add money as you go along, even $20 per month, you can dramatically increase those numbers.

So, back to the question of earning that kind of interest rate.

One thing is for sure; the banks (at least not in the current interest rate environment or anytime soon) are not paying that. As a general rule of thumb, the safer a particular savings or investment option, and the easier it is for you to get your money back at will, the lower the rate of return will be. Some banks pay higher interest rates than others, and generally, internet-based banks pay the highest of all since they do not have the overhead associated with maintaining physical locations. And while later I will speak to the importance of your primary bank having physical locations, that's not to say an internet bank is a bad choice to strictly keep your savings accounts. Electronic funds transfers are generally free and the money can be transferred to your main bank in as little as two days.

The main types of bank accounts where you can put your money are:

➢ **Checking** – Generally, they pay little to no interest and should only hold enough of your money to cover any upcoming bills.

➢ **Savings and money market accounts** – The interest rates are slightly higher than checking accounts and you can take money out whenever you wish, but since they are designed for savings they do impose limits on how many times per month you can withdraw funds. It is important to note that the restriction is on the *number* of transactions, not the *dollar amount,* so if you do need to withdraw money, make sure you plan accordingly and take enough in one or two transactions. For the specific rules about these limits, consult with the institution of your choosing or at www.fdic.gov.

➢ **Certificates of Deposit (CDs)** – These are like a savings account meets a contract with the bank. Savings rates can change at any time without notice, but with a CD you are agreeing to a set term (generally anywhere from three months to ten years), at a specified interest rate that is guaranteed for the length of the certificate. The positive of this option is that there is no mystery in what your interest rate will be, and if rates happen to drop you are protected. One negative is that if rates go up you will be locked into this existing lower rate and unable to move your money from this account to a new one. The other downside is that the bank oftentimes imposes penalties for withdrawing money prior to the maturity date, and those fees can range from simply forfeiting any interest earned to also losing a percentage of your initial deposit.

Outside of bank accounts, there are a few other options for investing your money that come with higher returns – but also with increased risk. Most of these options revolve around two types of investment vehicles, which I will describe briefly, as well as the other options they give rise to, but this is not meant to be a book on the mechanics of investing – simply to give you a basic understanding so that you can look into learning more on your own. There are numerous, very technical definitions for each that can be found online or in any investing book or magazine, but I am going to simplify them both to the most basic level.

➤ **Stock** - Is a share of ownership in a company. Want to become an owner of Apple? You can just buy shares of their stock and you now have a fractional ownership and can benefit from how well that business performs based on the price of that share increasing. Conversely, if Apple is not doing well those shares of stock can decrease in value. It is important to note, that you can sell your shares at any time, and that is when you will either *realize* the gain (by getting more money back than you invested) or the loss (getting back less money than you invested). Any changes in value before you sell are called "paper gains and losses" because you still own the shares and have not taken any money back.

➤ **Bond** – These are similar to stocks in that they are often issued by companies (but also by the city, state and federal government), only instead of owning a piece of that company you are actually becoming one of their creditors – simply meaning someone who has lent them money. Bonds have a specific time period they must be held for, and they guarantee you a certain interest rate (very similar to a CD). So, as long as you hold the bonds to maturity, and the company does not go out of business, you are guaranteed your initial investment back and will have collected dividend payments (the interest earned) along the way. Like a stock, you may be able to sell a bond prior to maturity, in which case you can either get back more or less than what you paid depending on how attractive the interest rate you are earning is.

It is important to note that the single largest difference between a stock and a bond is what happens to you if the company goes out of business. As a general rule of thumb, stockholders will get very little to none of their investment back in this scenario, and that is because they are last on the list of payees in bankruptcy court. Bondholders are given a higher priority since they are creditors and not owners, and there is a better chance of recouping some of their initial investment.

Have you ever heard the expression, "don't put all of your eggs in one basket?" Well just in case you haven't, it basically means that you should spread your risk around. The mechanics of buying individual stocks and bonds can be both expensive and tricky. If you only own one type of stock or bond, and the company goes bankrupt, you stand to lose everything. It was for this reason that mutual funds and exchange-traded funds (ETFs) were invented.

The basic concept is that your money gets lumped into a pool with money from other investors like yourself, and in many cases is managed by a professional who selects hundreds of different stocks and/or bonds in any one fund. So, every dollar you invest may buy you a penny's worth of Apple stock along with a number of other companies. These options, much like stocks and bonds, can earn you those rates that approach the 12% mark we spoke about earlier and can play a crucial part in your investment mix. More to come on this later as well when we get into discussing the different options you have for retirements plans offered through your employer.

The last thing to note on this topic is that there is only one correct choice for where to put your money, and that is everywhere! No, that's not a joke. The best way to maximize returns, minimize risk and avoid unnecessary fees is to own a combination of the bank and investment options previously mentioned. Any emergency fund money, or funds that you might need to withdraw in the next six months to one year, should be kept as liquid as possible. Yes, you won't earn nearly as much in interest, but you also won't run into a situation where you may have to liquidate an investment account that has lost money and turn those paper losses into real dollars and cents.

If you choose to work with a financial advisor, this is another area where you should do your homework first. Needless to say, like any professional, they do not work for free and their fees can vary wildly – oftentimes eating away at the returns you are using them to attain in the first place. When you are just starting out, it will most likely not be cost-effective for you or the adviser to work together as they are generally paid in one of three ways.

> **Flat fee** – More fitting for financial planners and not brokers, but they charge per hour, or possibly per year, and oftentimes send you off to do the legwork yourself after helping you develop a strategy.

> **Transaction based** – Any time an investment is bought or sold in your account, they generate a commission. The potential problem here is when their recommendations to buy and sell are solely based on padding their pockets and not on your financial well-being.

> **Fee-based** – They charge a percentage of your account value as a management fee, and that percentage is the same whether you make or lose money. Sure, it's in their best interest for your account to grow, because the higher the value the more dollars that same percentage equates to in their pocket. There is also a minimum account size they will handle.

The bottom line here is, with all of the information readily available today, you most likely won't need an advisor for quite some time – possibly never, if you enjoy finance and get good at learning the intricacies of investing early on in life. You can open an investment account at any number of websites or phone-based apps, from good old E-trade to newcomers like Robinhood. See who has more reasonable fees, better research tools, and the easier to use interface that suits your style and start there. Guess what? If you don't like it, much like banking, you are not locked in and can switch platforms at any time.

Interest Rate Research:

1) Using the resources provided, or your own research/preferred tools, create an average of rates for the following:

A. **Credit cards**
   Lowest rate:
   Highest Rate:
   Average Rate:

B. **Auto loans**
   Lowest rate:
   Highest Rate:
   Average Rate:

C. **Personal Loans**
   Lowest rate:
   Highest Rate:
   Average Rate:

D. **Mortgages**
   Lowest rate:
   Highest Rate:
   Average Rate:

2) Perform the same task you did above on accounts that will earn you interest:

A. **Checking**
   Lowest rate:
   Highest Rate:
   Average Rate:

B. **Savings/money market**
   Lowest rate:
   Highest Rate:
   Average Rate:

C. **CDs**
   Lowest rate:
   Highest Rate:
   Average Rate:

D. **Mutual Funds**
   Lowest rate:
   Highest Rate:
   Average Rate:

"Getting to a higher spiritual level is like increasing your credit score. You get a lot more points for sinning and repenting than if you have no credit history at all."

-Lisa Kleypas

Chapter 2: Credit Scores

This section is in no way meant to be a comprehensive guide to credit scores, but rather a bird's eye view to help you get familiar with the basics. Credit scores and the bureaus responsible for calculating and monitoring them are as elusive and confusing as quantum physics in my opinion. Entire books, countless articles, and numerous companies have been dedicated to helping people understand credit scores and how they work, so if you have a thirst for more knowledge after reading this I advise hitting the internet, local bookstore or library to get immersed.

The first thing to understand about your credit score is that you actually have three of them, and none is more important than another. There is no telling which of the three a bank or lender is going to use when you apply for a loan with them, and they will not look at a different one just because you show them that it is better than the one that they originally looked at. On major loan applications, like a mortgage, the lender may pull all three of your credit scores and will generally utilize the middle or lowest score in their decision on whether or not to approve you and to determine the interest rate you will pay.

The term "FICO score" has become synonymous with credit, much like Kleenex became the household name for a tissue. FICO actually stands for Fair Isaac and Company, named for the company that was a pioneer in the creation of credit scores much the same way Xerox was in office services. Each of the three bureaus named below will calculate your FICO score differently, though.

The three companies who handle credit reporting (Credit Bureaus) are Experian, Equifax, and Transunion. The typical score range for each of these reporting agencies is between 300 – 850. While not all information is reported the same to each, and the methodology behind how they calculate your score can vary, below is a fairly acceptable idea of what each score range is considered to be in the eyes of lenders.

300 – 629: Bad

630 – 689: Average

690 – 719: Good

720 – 850: Excellent

This may seem overwhelming if you have never dealt with credit before, so for simplicity's sake try to think in these terms. In order to get a mortgage backed by a government agency, as most are, you will need a minimum credit score of at least 620. If you want to put less than a 25% down payment, that minimum score jumps to 680. It is commonly believed that banks, credit card issuers, and finance companies reserve their lowest rates for folks who have a credit score of at least 720. So as long as you are responsible with credit and take the necessary steps to safeguard yourself, the score will naturally increase over time.

There are a ton of resources out there about credit. Everywhere you turn there are commercials, advertisements and third party companies trying to help you build or repair your credit – at a cost, of course. This actually goes for Experian, Equifax, and Transunion as well. When you visit their websites, they have plenty of great information, but also a number of services that you can sign up for, sometimes with very hefty monthly fees attached. Even the companies out there like Credit Karma and Freecreditreport.com that advertise free credit scores have tricky ways of getting you to sign up for additional paid services after the trial period ends, or automatically billing for a subscription if you do not cancel it yourself. What many people do not realize is that there is no need to fall victim to any of these traps that prey on your fears of having poor credit. I am going to list four sites below, one for each of the credit bureaus, and the last one for the government-sponsored site that allows you to obtain a free, no strings attached copy of your credit report from all three bureaus every twelve months. Should you need any further knowledge in this area, these would be the best places to start:

www.experian.com

www.equifax.com

www.transunion.com

www.annualcreditreport.com

A big misconception is that credit is dangerous. I can't count how many times in my life that someone has said, "I don't do credit," or "only cash for me." This mentality is going to do yourself a tremendous disservice as life goes on and you want to make more expensive purchases, such as a car or a house, which most normal people cannot afford to do in one lump sum of cash. In today's modern society, having no credit can actually be worse than bad credit. When you have bad credit, there is a clear path to fix it. Start paying your bills on time, clean up those delinquent balances and monitor your score. Having no credit history at all is a Catch-22. No one wants to offer you credit because you have no track record of responsibility, and you cannot prove you are responsible unless someone takes a chance by giving you credit.

So what is one to do in this situation? There are a few options that I can offer as a way to avoid winding up with this problem:

The first is to be added as an "authorized user" on a family member's credit card. You have no liability for paying the bill, and as such, this can be risky for whoever adds you to their account, but it does start to build your credit in a minimalistic way and is the easiest option. The person who adds you does not even have to give you access to the physical credit card. The sole fact that your name and social security number are attached to it will offer you some of the benefits from their responsible usage. An important thing to note here, though, is that an "authorized user" is very different from becoming a "joint cardholder." In that scenario, you would need to be approved much the same as if applying on your own and you will be fully liable for every charge and payment.

Another option is to apply for a "secured" credit card or personal loan. This is where the bank will ask you for a deposit before issuing a credit card. Sometimes, that deposit can be 100% of your credit line, meaning they hold $500 of your money then allow you to spend up to $500 on the card. Other times, your deposit will only be a portion of your credit line. With a secured loan, the bank is holding your money and then lending it back to you with interest. I know, after the whole last chapter on interest rates why would you want to pay for a loan you don't need? The main reason is to prove that you are financially responsible, and every timely payment you make toward that loan will build your credit history. Other reasons may include not having the discipline to replace your emergency fund and making loan payments can be a sort of forced savings, but we won't waste too much time on those reasons.

Another misconception about credit scores is that only late or missed payments negatively affect you. As I mentioned earlier, there are countless factors that can impact your credit score. This is not an all-inclusive list, but some factors that can hurt you are:

➤ Using too much of your credit limit per credit card.

➤ Using too much of your overall credit limit.

> ➤ The amount you owe in relation to your available credit limits.

> ➤ Closing an account that you have had for a very long time.

> ➤ Having too much credit available at any one time.

> ➤ Opening too many new accounts in a short period of time.

> ➤ Having too many open accounts.

> ➤ Having too many applications for credit or inquiries into your credit report in a short period of time.

Utilizing the tools mentioned in this section to check your credit report on a regular basis is highly advisable. You do not need to become neurotic about it, checking once a year should be sufficient in most cases. There is no penalty or adverse effect to checking your own credit score, however anytime another party (such as a bank or finance company) makes an inquiry you will lose points. That is not to say you should never apply for anything, but that you should do so selectively. All inquiries from a third party that happen within a thirty-day period are generally treated as the same inquiry. The reason for that is because when you are in the market for a large purchase, such as a car or a home, in order to make sure you are getting the best rate you will want to shop around and it would be unfair if your score dropped each time. Just be mindful to make sure you are ready to proceed when you start this process so that your credit is not being pulled again after the thirty days.

Another important thing to think about when checking your credit report is the question of what exactly you are looking for. While knowing your score can be helpful, the bigger advantage is in reviewing the accounts that appear under your social security number. If you only have one credit card, and your credit report shows that you have two or more that could be a sign of potential fraud. Should you ever encounter something like this, the first thing you want to look for is if the account listed has a phone number for the provider so that you can contact them for more information. Sometimes, one company may buy another and that is the reason for a duplicate listing. But if there is no contact information, or contacting the company does not put your mind at ease then you can file a dispute directly with the credit bureau, usually through their website or contacting their customer service phone number for explicit instructions.

The bottom line is that your credit history, or lack thereof, will be with you for the rest of your life. Unless you plan on living on an island or going off the grid completely, your credit score is one of, if not the most important pieces of your adult financial life. Mistakes happen, life can be complicated; there is no question about it. In the grand scheme of a robust credit history, a missed payment here and going over your credit limit there will not set you on the path to ruin. But becoming a habitual late payer, or spending more than you have, will start to make it more and more daunting to recover from. Credit cards also offer a host of other benefits, which we will cover in more detail later.

One last thing to note on credit scores is that the three companies responsible for reporting this data are not infallible. They are not actively involved in checking the accuracy of the items reported on individual credit reports, instead they are merely the "middle-man" if you will. All types of creditors submit data to the bureaus based on your repayment history with them. In this process there is ample opportunity for human error to occur. Maybe a digit in a social security number was mistyped or transposed, the report was supposed to be for someone with your name but a different middle initial, or countless other scenarios where an honest mistake can cause havoc for you. The silver lining in this cloud, though, is that you do have rights to challenge erroneous findings through a dispute process. Each company will have instructions on their website detailing how to go about doing this, but if you ever find yourself in doubt you can always reach out to a professional or look for my upcoming instructional guide on how to handle it yourself with confidence.

Credit Score Accountability:

1) Go to annualcreditreport.com to review your three credit reports and use this space to keep track of your findings:

<u>Bureau</u>   <u>Notes</u>

A. Experian:

B. Equifax:

C. Transunion:

2) Use a site you are comfortable with to obtain your credit scores and list them below:

A. Experian:

B. Equifax:

C. Transunion:

3) What are some things you can do to increase your credit score if need be?

4) Research what you need to do to in order to dispute erroneous records on your credit report:

"Everything in life is somewhere else, and you get there in a car."

-E. B. White

Chapter 3: Your First Car

To stick with the current theme of credit and interest rates, this is a great time to circle back to the earlier topic of auto loans. As we established earlier, most of us need to be able to drive in order to accomplish dozens of tasks we may take for granted until we have no wheels. And as with most things in life, there are choices that must be made when deciding how to go about getting your vehicle. There are additional expenses that come with owning a car beyond just the monthly payment options we will discuss. Some of those are gas, insurance and maintenance, so before deciding which car option is right for you, first think about whether you really need one at the moment or if it would be better to save money and keep using other options until you are in a better place financially.

Once you are certain that public transportation and chauffeured trips from mom and dad are not going to cut it anymore, it is time to decide if you want a new or used car. I know, I know. Who doesn't want to drive a new car, right? While it undoubtedly makes us feel good to zip around town in the newest model of your favorite car, it does not always make the most financial sense. As soon as a new car is driven off the dealership lot, it is immediately worth less than what you paid for it. By now you probably think I am crazy, but unfortunately, that is just another painful reality oftentimes overlooked. If you wreck your new car the day you bought it, your insurance company will most likely not pay the full purchase price unless you bought additional coverage, known as GAP insurance.

One of the first things you will want to do, regardless of which option is the best, is figure out how much money you can afford to spend on the vehicle of choice. There is a chapter later on that will cover budgeting in depth, so if that is an area you struggle with then I highly advise skipping there first before continuing this chapter. Outside of a housing payment, the monthly cost of a car is often the second highest expenditure most Americans make. There is nothing worse than falling in love with a particular car and then realizing you can't afford it, or worse, convincing yourself that you can and then getting stuck in a tough situation.

The cost of the car is not the only thing you should be concerned with, either. The cost of car insurance varies wildly from one type of car to another and can easily become a deal breaker on your favorite vehicle. Call an insurance agent to get specific quotes before ever setting foot in a dealership to save you a lot of pain later on. The same can be said for the amount of research that you put in to the numerous different options in your price range before ever setting foot in a dealership. There are so many online resources for information on cars that there is no excuse not to have a clue instead of just trusting what the salesperson tells you. No one will ever care as much about the car you will be stuck with for the next few years than you do.

New Cars

With all of that said, let's say you decide that the new car option is still the road for you. It is important to know the three ways you can go about making that happen. We already spoke about the first option, which is paying in full, and how unlikely that is for most of us starting out. If you can swing it, that's great. That is one less monthly payment to make and a huge interest savings over the life of ownership.

The next choice would be to finance the car, so think back to everything that we just learned about interest rates, as they will apply here. Not only will this option cost you more money than buying outright, it also comes with a few other pitfalls. For starters, you will most likely own and/or be making payments on this vehicle for more years than your manufacturer's warranty covers. As cars get older, things tend to break. Once outside of the warranty period, all of those headaches will become yours, at your own expense. Also, life changes and you may be stuck with a vehicle that no longer meets your needs a few years down the road. The biggest benefit of financing though, is that at some point – provided you didn't wreck or sell the car – you will reach a point where it is paid for in full and the payments cease. You can then save money every month by continuing to drive it and pocketing that payment, or sell it and use that money toward the purchase of a new vehicle.

The final, and one of the most common options these days is to lease your new car. Leasing is basically a long-term rental car for lack of a simpler way of explaining it. You are still liable for the same sales taxes and other administrative fees just as if you bought the car, and in most cases these are due upfront never to be seen again. That is pitfall number one of leasing.

Then, you drive and make your payments for the next 24 to 39 months, depending on your lease agreement, and return the car. At this point, you are left back in the same situation you started out in, with no car and a decision to make. Sure, the dealer will allow you to purchase that car at the end of the lease, but now you are basically buying a used car – used by you, but used all the same. And your monthly payments could now be as much, if not more, than when you were paying for the same car when it was brand new. Most people tend to just lease again at the end of the term, which is great because you are always driving a relatively new car, but also bad because at that rate you will have an auto loan payment to make for the rest of your life.

Whether or not you think you will ever want to buy that car at the end of the lease period, it is best to negotiate what the resale value will be before entering into the lease at all. The reason for this is because the future purchase price is stipulated at lease signing. If something changes and you wind up wanting or needing to buy that car three years later, you will no longer have any leverage to negotiate that price. You might even have more flexibility at this time to secure a lower price in the future as the dealership is more concerned with making a sale in the present and knows the odds of you cashing in on that lower price later are slim to none, especially when they can just entice you with offers on a new lease.

One last point to make on leasing a car that will hopefully never happen to you, but carries such far-reaching consequences it is worth noting. If the person who leased a vehicle passes away, that contract with the finance company does not become voided. They will expect a family member or the estate of the deceased party to continue making payments until the maturity date. This is especially true if you have co-signed on a lease for someone else. Even if you have your own car and do not have the financial means to make these payments it will be held against your credit report as a delinquent account. This is actually one of the most popular complaints that news outlets get in regards to investigating unfair business practices. Unfortunately, you cannot change a legally binding contract after the fact, so it is best to be informed upfront of your potential risks and responsibilities.

Used Cars

Now that we are all experts on the pros and cons of new car ownership, let's move on to the used car option. Your first choice here is the same as with a new car – to pay cash – and that may make more sense in this instance. For starters, the prices of used cars are generally far lower than new ones, making it more realistic. Also, the interest rates on used car loans tend to be higher than on new cars, making financing more costly in the long run. Since a used car is more likely to need frequent upkeep and maintenance than a new car, you can put away a portion of the money that would have gone to the car payment each month into an emergency fund to be better prepared to pay for those situations when they arise.

I recently learned that leasing also happens to be an option for a used car, a concept that is difficult to wrap my head around. You will have to pay the same upfront taxes and fees that you would with a new car lease. For the next two or three years, you will be renting a car that is two to four years old, and when the lease period expires you have the option of leasing again or now buying out the twice used car. This option may make sense in certain instances, but definitely do your homework first and see just how much cheaper it is to lease used instead of new before committing.

Financing that used car is the final option. This is also where I would advise performing the most due diligence. The term "used car salesman" has had a terrible connotation for almost as long as used cars have been sold, and usually for good reason. Generally, people seeking out used, especially very used, low priced cars, do not have the credit, financial means, or savvy to purchase new cars. This makes them prime targets for unscrupulous car lots that need to move vehicles without concern for their customers. Yes, there are still the benefits of lower payments, avoiding depreciation, and even reduced insurance premiums, but caution should always be exercised – particularly in the area of the financing fine print and short-term warranty policy. The older the car, the more potential for breakage and mechanical failure, so having the ability to have it checked out by an independent mechanic before becoming stuck with it can be of paramount importance.

Miscellaneous Facts & Figures

Continuing with the topic of cars, I feel it is important to point out that financing and mechanical issues are not the only areas where a dealership might try to profit from your naivety. It may be hard to believe, but dealers do not make a huge profit when they sell a car. In fact, oftentimes dealers will sell a car at a loss to move inventory and try to make money on other areas of the sale. If you don't believe me, just take a look at the advertisements where cars are being offered under MSRP (manufacturer's suggested retail price), or even under dealer invoice, which is what the dealer paid the manufacturer to purchase that vehicle. Would you buy something for $2 and turn around to sell it for $1? Of course not, but there is a method to their madness.

We spoke about finance charges and lease payments, which when offered through their own finance companies, makes them a profit every time a payment is made in the form of the interest you are paying. They can afford to lose money upfront so long as they know they can turn a profit by the end of your term. And, you took the hit on the depreciation when you drove it home. But dealers often offer a number of extras when you are completing your paperwork. For those of you yet to encounter this part of the process it is by far the most uncomfortable, borderline sleazy, moment of the sales experience. You agree to everything with your salesperson and are then whisked away to a back room where the Finance Manager has a chance to review all of the details with you.

In this backroom, any number of things is bound to happen. And while this is not exclusive to used cars, it is more common. I've purchased my fair share of new and used cars, as well as leased, so this room is no mystery to me and still gives me anxiety despite all of that experience. I have personally been asked to sign paperwork that did not match what I agreed to, and when this was pointed out to the Finance Manager, it was laughed off as a mistake then reprocessed – only to be incorrect yet again. This is one of the subtle ways they will try to make more money off of you. Once you sign that agreement and walk out the door, most errors or deceit become binding.

A less subtle way is when you are informed that your monthly payment is higher than expected because of an issue with your credit score or the amount of your down payment. Starting to make sense as to why I covered these areas earlier? In these situations, the best thing you can do is threaten to walk away. Never let on as to how badly you want or need the car in question or they will play on your emotions to get their way. A great way to do this is to say that you will check with your own bank and get back to them. They know that most people who walk out their doors never return.

They also know that much of their profit is made from financing the car themselves, so you going to your bank and finding out that they were lying will cost them that profit at best, and the whole deal at worst. Once you utter these words, that Finance Manager will feverishly get to work on his computer and many times miraculously let you know he was able to make it happen for you. Depending on your conviction level and their scruples in this department, they may try to make one or two more offers before settling on what you were originally promised, so stick to your guns and get what you and the salesperson agreed to.

Another classic tactic of Finance Managers is to try and sell you a bunch of stuff you don't really need at a price they can't justify. Let's take an extended warranty for example. This is my favorite when it comes to a lease since most of, if not all, that time you will be covered by the manufacturer's warranty (usually 36,000 miles or 3 years and even higher for some brands like Hyundai and Kia). The only time this could potentially be beneficial is if you have a 39-month lease, but even then you are paying extra money every month for something that may only be useful in the last three months.

I have witnessed attempts at selling tire insurance. That's right, where they reimburse you for expenses associated with flat tires.

Grow Up!

The problems with this type of coverage are that:

> Over the life of the loan, your tire insurance premium can cost more than if you just paid out of pocket to replace all of the tires yourself.

> The fine print on what was or was not covered −such as excessive wear and tear − was so extensive there was probably no chance of them ever paying out anyway.

> You may have to get the tires directly from them, severely limiting your options if stranded on the side of the road with a flat.

Roadside assistance is another one of my favorite scams. Even if the car is for an elderly parent, new teen driver, or your pregnant wife − this option almost never makes sense. They will play on your emotions, possibly even make you feel guilty in front of said loved one, but do not fall for it. AAA (Automobile Association of America) is still a cheaper and more reliable option than brand-specific plans. And, if that wasn't enough to convince you, AAA will also cover any car that you own or happen to be a passenger in for one low annual fee, whereas the dealer plan will only cover that specific vehicle.

There is one last area to be extremely careful with when it comes to the fine print in car contracts, and that is with the "end of lease" agreement. Remember, when you lease a car it is like a long-term rental. The dealership expects that vehicle back in a very specific – good – condition.

When you agree to lease a car, the first thing that can cost you a boatload of money is the number of miles you are allowed to drive per year. This number generally ranges from 7,500 to 15,000. Often times, you will see advertisements for such low lease payments that it seems unbelievable, and the reason for that is that price is usually followed by the words "low mileage lease." Depending where you live, 7,500 miles may not even be enough to cover your daily commute to and from work, let alone everything else you expect to do with your car. When you return the car with additional mileage, the penalties can range from $.10 to $.25 per mile. So, if you drove 20,000 miles in a two-year lease, you could wind up owing $500 to $1,250 in penalties – and that is with only driving an extra 2,500 miles per year. Needless to say, the bill can become very expensive very quickly.

The other area that can become costly when you return the car is any excess "wear and tear." Dealerships have very specific guidelines on what is acceptable when it comes to all aspects of your car's appearance. Nicks, dings and dents, depending on the size, can all wind up coming out of your pocket. Stains or tears on the interior upholstery or leather will have a price tag as well. The specifications are so strict that they will even inspect how much of the tread is left on your tires. So, if you held off on buying new tires for a while because money was tight and you knew the lease was expiring soon anyway, the joke will wind up being on you. There will be a charge for new tires, and you will have no say over which brand they choose and the bill associated with it.

All of these expensive pitfalls can also turn into another area where you do have some room to negotiate, though. Many dealerships will reduce or waive some of these penalties if they have the chance to keep your business. Maybe you plan on leasing again and have not decided where or what yet. If they can get you into another one of their cars they are much more willing to overlook these items. Also, if you want to buy the car outright at the end of the lease, the penalties will be avoided – you just now own the car with all of the excess wear and tear.

At the end of the day, if you know you have no intention of working with that dealership again, have the foresight to repair as many of these issues yourself as possible before returning the car. In fact, most dealerships will allow you to bring the car in a few weeks or months before your lease is up so that they can inspect it and give you an itemized list of what is wrong and what the associated charges will be. Take advantage of that opportunity!

<u>Car Buying Tool:</u>

1) Figure out how much you can afford per month and write it here:

2) Use an auto loan calculator (https://www.calculator.net/loan-calculator.html) to determine the maximum purchase price of a car you can afford (try not to go longer than 60 months). It is not always worth it if the loan outlives the car.

3) Which option seems to suit you better?

    -New   -Used

        -Purchase or Lease

4) Research lease prices and how much money is required as a down payment. Inquire what the new payment would be with less money down if you are strapped for cash.

5) Identify three vehicles that fit your budget:

6) Call your insurance company and ask for a quote on each to see if they still fit in your budget:

"The ache for home lies in all of us, the safe place where we can go as we are and not be questioned."

-Maya Angelou

Chapter 4: Adult Living Options

Living at home with your parents or other extended family members can be a drag. Even if you have a great relationship with them, sometimes it can feel that you are unable to grow or expand your horizons in the ways that you would like. At some point, at least for those who don't want to be forty years old living in their parents' basement, moving out will become necessary. This can seem incredibly daunting, or it should anyway providing you have given it any type of thought and don't just decide to pack up and go one day. Having your own place can become very expensive in the blink of an eye. The longer you are able to bear living at home where you hopefully do not pay rent, or are paying far less than you would in your own place, the better off you will be in the long run.

If your goal is to own your own home one day, paying rent can make it impossible to save enough money to accomplish that. That is just one decision to think about. Maybe you want to have roommates to help share in the expenses, which sounds like a prudent move at face value. That could consist of living with a complete stranger or possibly someone you thought you knew very well. When I first moved out, I had one from each category. My first two roommates were my brother and a friend of his I did not know very well. I will spare you the extensive details of all the ways that arrangement failed, just know that at the end of our first year we decided it best to go our separate ways while everyone was still on speaking terms.

I share this only so that others can hopefully learn from some of the things that seemed like a good idea at the time in my own life, only to wind up costing me far more than they saved in the long run. Roommate or not, there are two basic options you have when it is time to move out and we will discuss those in detail now.

Renting

My first word of caution here is to try to get your parents' or family's blessing before you do. Unless you have already mastered the credit score game and have a great paying job that will look attractive on paper to potential landlords, you just might need their help. Landlords are not so different from banks, credit card companies and other lenders in the fact that they want to be sure they are dealing with someone who is financially responsible. The difference, at least in many instances, is that landlords are not corporate behemoths who can absorb missed payments. When you rent an apartment in a two-family home, and your landlord relies on that payment to help cover their mortgage and feed their family, you better believe they are going to be very selective in who they rent to.

Before we even get into the subject of the actual lease terms and conditions, it is important to understand what a landlord will be expecting from you in order to even be considered. It has been mentioned enough times already that there should be no surprise when I say that a credit check will be performed. And, unlike other regulated areas of lending – like mortgages and credit cards – where lenders set a minimum acceptable score, there is not always a way of knowing what your prospective landlord considers "acceptable." And just because you meet the credit requirements does not mean you are guaranteed acceptance.

The next thing almost always required is proof of income – physical proof. Your word on how much you make is not going to cut it. Paystubs covering the last two weeks to two months will be the documents required. This leads to a question that will be answered later, but I want to quickly mention it in case you fall into the category of someone who works "off the books." You may make great money in this type of arrangement, but lose the ability to provide the necessary proof of said earnings. Moving back to requirements, landlords may also require you to provide references from prior landlords so that they can find out what kind of tenant you were. This can be the easiest one to skirt because there is no way they can prove that you ever actually rented from the person whose name you provide – that could just be your cousin.

While renting an apartment is definitely cheaper than trying to buy something in most markets, it is not as cheap as commonly believed. Once a landlord accepts your rental application, there will be the business of signing the lease agreement to tend to. One of the first items covered in this document is the amount of monthly rent and how much money you must provide the landlord upfront – a number that typically represents a combination of prepaid rent and a security deposit.

This requirement can vary widely by location and landlord. But for illustrative purposes, let's say that the monthly rent is $1,000 and the lease calls for the first month's rent and one-month security deposit upfront. That means that you must pay the landlord $2,000 when you sign; $1,000 will cover the rent for your first month and the other $1,000 will be held in escrow in case you damage the apartment or default on your lease. It is not uncommon to be asked for one-month rent and two months' security, so now that same scenario has you shelling out $3,000, $2,000 of which cannot be used toward any following month's rent and you will not regain access to it until you move out, provided you have kept the apartment in great condition.

Now that you have saved up your money, proved your worth to the landlord and set your sights on a new future of independence, there is the most important part of all to tend to – reading the remainder of the lease agreement and being aware of what you are signing. A common misconception is that you can do whatever you want in your new place since you are paying rent, but nothing can be further from the truth. I have witnessed some lease agreements that make the rules at good old mom and dad's place seem lenient. Some possible restrictions that you may encounter, and possibly want to address with your landlord before signing the lease, are listed below:

➢ No pets: This is a given in the majority of lease agreements. No matter how much you love your pet and swear that it is well behaved, there is an inherent risk to the landlord. Dogs can bite people and damage property. Cat dander is incredibly difficult to remove, especially from carpet, and should there be other tenants nearby with an allergy or prospective future tenants when you move out, it will pose an issue for the landlord. Sometimes cats are more widely accepted than dogs, so you may be able to plead a case for that. And even if dogs are accepted, it is very likely that a restriction will be put on the size and breed – oftentimes as required by the landlord's homeowner's insurance company. The bottom line is if you have a pet make sure to fully disclose that upfront and only look for apartments advertising that pets are allowed so as not to wind up disappointed, or worse, in violation of your lease.

➢ Guests: If you live in a private residence as opposed to an apartment building, it is not unheard of for restrictions to be placed on how many people you can entertain. Parties or large gatherings are generally banned outright, for obvious reasons. But I know of some landlords who have gone as far as to prohibit having any guests spending the night. That kind of limitation can really put a cramp on your bachelor or bachelorette lifestyle.

➢ Property upkeep: It is no longer safe to assume that the landlord is always responsible for routine chores such as cutting the grass or shoveling the snow. Read carefully so you know what is expected of you, and potentially use this area to earn yourself a discounted rent payment by offering to handle some of these tasks for the landlord, especially if they do not live onsite.

➢ Utilities: There is no standard in this department that I know of and we will discuss it a little more in the next section covering unexpected expenses. But the basic utilities to be aware of are: heat, hot water, water, and electricity. All to none of these could be included and knowing that upfront will assist you with budgeting for them.

Since we just went over the topic of utilities as they pertain to leases and whose responsibility they are, it is only fitting to move into the last topic involved in renting your own place – unexpected expenses. If you were used to living in a household where someone else took care of all the expenses and luxuries that you're accustomed to, it can be a shock to find out what you are going to pay in addition to rent. Electricity alone can run $100 per month or more if you live in a climate that requires air-conditioning to be used most of the year. Heat and hot water can easily run the same, or more in the winter if you are in a colder climate. And that's all before you tack on the additional services of cable television, Internet and the obligatory Netflix subscription. It would be wise to assume an extra $500 will be needed on top of your monthly rent to ensure you aren't living in the dark or bored out of your mind.

When we covered auto loans and mortgages, we spoke about those unpleasant scenarios where you are unable to pay your bills and the different ways the bank could go about taking their property back. That same principle applies to your newly furnished apartment. Rules vary from city to city when it comes to tenant-landlord disputes for non-payment of rent. There are cities such as New York City (Manhattan and the other boroughs) that are tenant-friendly, making it seem like renters have more rights than the people who actually own the apartment and the eviction process can take six months or longer (not trying to give you any ideas). But there are plenty of other places where a landlord can have a tenant evicted as quickly as thirty days after the first missed payment.

It is important to know that this is not a cordial process where someone will help you load your belongings and move out with a parting handshake. Most likely, you will come home to find an eviction notice from a local Marshall or Sheriff, the door locks changed and your belongings forfeited. That's right, you are not just homeless at this point, but also out whatever furniture, electronics or other personal property you may hold dear. Even if you are under a lease for another six, twelve or eighteen months, the moment you realize paying rent may be a challenge it is best to have a discussion with your landlord about breaking the lease. Most will welcome your honesty and appreciate you saving them the legal headache of an eviction proceeding, some may even waive any penalties and return your security deposit provided the place was left in good condition and you give at least enough notice for them to find a new tenant.

Mortgages

Okay, let's up the ante for a minute. Either you have rented for a while and are ready to graduate to home ownership, or you were diligent enough to save a down payment while living at home and plan to skip renting altogether. The process of getting a mortgage can be one of the single most stressful things a person does in their life, even moreso if you have no idea what to expect. And this is one of those tricky subjects to ask others about because so much has changed in the rules and regulations governing mortgages since the financial crisis of 2008, that anyone who has not gone through the process since then will not be aware of.

The first point to make is that there is no such thing as

buying a house with no down payment, something that was commonplace prior to 2008. In order to qualify for a conventional mortgage, a 20% down payment is required. So if the home costs $200,000, you would need to have $40,000 on hand for a deposit. There are other mortgage programs out there that will allow you to put down less (anywhere from 3% to 10%) but these are not conventional options and come with other catches and expenses. Whenever you put less than 20% down, you are likely to be given a higher interest rate, which as we all know by now, means higher monthly payments and more money spent over the life of the loan.

The biggest pitfall of putting less than 20% down is an ugly add-on the mortgage companies charge you, called PMI (private mortgage insurance). This is not insurance that you benefit from in any way, shape or form. It is actually a policy that the bank takes out to ensure against you defaulting on your mortgage, and you get the honor of paying the premiums every month for them to have that protection. Now your monthly payment just went up to the tune of hundreds of dollars for something you gain nothing from at all. To make matters worse, this PMI payment will remain with you until you reach 20% equity in your home – a feat that is subjective (think back to how little of your monthly payment actually goes toward principal every month), and must be approved by the bank before the payments can stop. PMI is by far the worst expense to incur when buying a home.

For illustrative purposes, let's quickly think about what

"equity" is as used for the purpose of PMI. Equity is essentially the amount of your home that you actually own. If your home is valued at $200,000 and you put down $40,000 as a down payment, that $40,000 is your equity. After 10 years, let's pretend your house is now worth $250,000 and you owe a balance of $175,000. You now have $75,000 (more actually depending on how much principal you have paid down but we will keep it simple) equity in your home, which translates to approximately 43% ($75,000/$175,000). Because there are so many factors involved in calculating exactly how much equity you may have in the home at any point in time, it is more than likely the PMI will not be removed earlier than what was stipulated at closing and another reason why it should be avoided.

Now that we have an idea of how much money you should have on hand to purchase in the most financially responsible way, let's move on to all of the other requirements you will need to meet. In the United States, most residential mortgages are regulated by the federal government through a number of different agencies. That means the government sets the requirements you must abide by and not the bank. It does not matter how many relatives you have working for banks or mortgage companies, there is nothing they can do to bypass the necessary documentation. Here is a list of what you will need to provide in almost all instances, and from every party on the loan. (All applicants must provide the same documents and must both have acceptable credit scores. If one person makes all of the money but has bad credit, and one has good credit and no income, the chances of the loan getting approved drop substantially.)

➢ Most recent 2 years tax returns (with W2's)

➢ Most recent pay stubs showing 30 days of pay*

➢ Proof of down payment**

➢ Bank account and investment statements for the last 60 days***

➢ The bank's application completed in full

➢ A completed request for IRS transcripts

➢ A most recent credit report that the bank will pull

* The lender will also call to verify employment, so quitting or changing jobs during the mortgage process can become a deal killer. It is also important to note that you may not have pay stubs if you are self-employed. Work with your lender to see what they will accept in lieu of these. Oftentimes, you can run financial reporting for the business through bookkeeping software like QuickBooks to generate what they will need. 2 years of your business tax returns will also most likely be requested in this scenario as well. ** Typically speaking, the money you are planning on using for the

down payment must be in your bank account for 60 days prior to your mortgage application. If not, the bank will require an explanation as to where the funds came from. Sometimes down payments are given by parents or family members as gifts, which is perfectly acceptable so long as they are willing to fill out a "gift letter" and provide bank statements of their own to prove that they had the funds for at least 60 days prior to the application.

*** Also important to mention is that, in this day and age, lenders are increasingly wary of cash transactions. When your bank statements are reviewed, any and all deposits for that 60-day period are subject to question. I have watched entire deals fall apart due to cash deposits that could not be explained. And no, working "off the books" is not an acceptable excuse. If you do deposit cash regularly for whatever reason, do yourself a favor and stop! Either use the cash to pay a bill directly so that it does not show up on your statements, keep it hidden in your house until after closing if you can afford to do so, or go to the Post Office and convert the cash to money orders before depositing. The $1 fee for the money order is a bargain considering the headaches you will save. Trust me, you will kick yourself for ignoring that piece of advice.

If that does not seem overwhelming enough yet, it's time to dive a little deeper into some of the other expenses that will be incurred in both the buying process and after you are officially a homeowner. Anything spent in the process of buying the house is generally done through your lender and are referred to as "closing costs." Depending where the property is located, these expenses can range from thousands to tens of thousands of dollars and are mandatory. All of these charges, or at least reasonable estimates of, will be disclosed to you upfront on a Good Faith Estimate or Loan Estimate, as required by federal law.

Some of these expenses can include:

➢ Appraisal fee

➢ Application fee

➢ Origination fee

➢ Inspection fee

➢ Legal fees

➢ Recording fees

➢ Prepaid real estate taxes

➢ Homeowner's insurance payment

➢ State mortgage tax

➢ Points, if any*

➢ Title search

➢ Title Insurance

> ➤ HOA fees**

> ➤ Prepaid Interest

> ➤ Underwriting fee

*Of all those fees just mentioned, I would like to single out what points are, also often referred to as "buying down the rate." Every point is 1% of the total loan amount that must be paid upfront, and will generally reduce your interest rate by .25%. In order to know if this makes sense for you, the lender will need to confirm exactly how much they will discount the rate for each point you purchase. You must also consider the possibility of using the money that would have purchased the point to increase your down payment and see which of the two saves you the most money in the long run. Let's take a look at some examples of how this might work.

Buying one point on a $160,000 loan at 5% will cost you $1,600 upfront but lower your interest rate to 4.75% for the life of the loan. In this example, we are assuming that the lender discounted the rate by .25%, your purchase price is $200,000 and that you are putting $40,000 down.

Here is what your various monthly payments and total interest paid over the life of the loan may look like:

A: Not buying any points and taking the standard rate.

Example: $160,000 @ 5% = $859/month, with total interest paid of $149,209.

B: Spending $1,600 on the point, which is added into the total interest paid.

Example: $160,000 @ 4.75% = $835/month, with total interest paid of $142,069.

C: Using the $1,600 to increase the down payment.

Example: $158,400 @ 5% = $850/month, with total interest paid of $146,117.

Which of the three do you think is the better option? In this example, it does seem that Option B, or buying the point, will give you the lowest monthly payment and also save you the most money in interest over the life of the loan. But please do not assume that means it will work the same every time. Loan amount, interest rate, and the size of the rate discount the point buys you all determine whether or not it makes sense. I used a simple mortgage calculator on Google to come up with these numbers so you do not need to be a mathematician, but you do need to be informed and diligent.

**HOA stands for Homeowners Association. These can come in many shapes and sizes, and until recently I actually did not realize just how prevalent they are in many parts of the country. When you purchase a home, it can come in the form of several different classifications that are not always explained up front, and each comes with its own benefits and pitfalls. Before making any final decision on what and where to purchase, it is best to always ask your realtor if there are any other fees such as these associated with the home. HOA fees can also be called "common charges" or "maintenance charges," but they all mean virtually the same thing.

There is the run-of-the-mill "house" where what you see is what you get, but you should be aware of the following designations as well:

➢ Co-op, or cooperative apartment as it is formally known, is predominantly a New York property type. In this type of arrangement you do not physically own the apartment you live in, rather shares in the building where it is housed. All residents share in the upkeep of the building, known as maintenance fees (HOA), and these can change with little notice based on the votes from the management "board." In this type of ownership you tend to feel more like a tenant and not an owner.

➢ Condo, or condominium, and townhouses are another type of housing where you are part of a greater association. Condos can be in either an apartment building type of layout or freestanding like a town house. There are fewer regulations in these units than there are in a co-op but there are still maintenance or HOA fees that must be paid.

➢ Private or gated communities are the last, and least obvious where you will encounter these HOA fees. These exist everywhere, from within cities to rural areas. You may be out in the middle of nowhere, nestled between nothing but trees and never expect to be part of a larger community. But nothing can be further from the truth. Many times locations like this make it a necessary evil for homeowners to form these associations to account for services that the local and state governments do not provide. Think snow plowing, road repair and other emergency maintenance issues.

The other two expenses to note are the real estate taxes and homeowner's insurance. When you buy a house, you have the option of escrowing these payments every month. This means that your total tax and insurance bill for the year is divided by 12 and then added to your monthly mortgage payment. Taxes and insurance are generally not due every month, so you are in effect letting the bank hold your money and earn interest on it every month, and in turn, they are responsible for paying these bills when they are due. In my opinion, there are only two good reasons to do this as opposed to making these payments yourself and controlling your cash flow better.

The first reason would be if the mortgage company offers you a better rate to allow them to escrow, or if they are going to charge you a higher rate for not letting them escrow, both situations that could realistically happen. The reason they would do this is to ensure that those payments are made and to protect their asset – your house. When property taxes go unpaid, the city or town can step in and place a lien on your property, with the ultimate option of selling that property out from under you, something that would not be in the bank's best interests.

The other reason this might make sense is if you know that keeping track of bills and managing money can be a struggle, possibly running the risk of becoming one of the situations the bank wants to avoid. In terms of unpaid insurance premiums, your policy could lapse. God forbid something happens to your house during this period and the insurance company will not pay the claim, possibly leaving the mortgage company on the hook without you paying them.

Everything that was just covered is only the major expected costs that will go into home ownership. There is also lawn care, snow removal, electricity, sanitation (yes, in many rural areas you must pay for that), heating, water, sewer, and countless other little and not so little expenses that will come up from time to time. Maintenance and repair of broken mechanical systems, plumbing, interior and exterior structural and cosmetic issues can add up in the blink of an eye and there is no landlord to call – all of that is your responsibility and expense. The bottom line here is, do not bite off more than you can chew when it comes to your monthly housing payment. Make sure your monthly income does not only cover the monthly housing payment and your other household expenses like food, cell phones, etc., but that you leave a comfortable amount to set aside in case of emergencies.

To stress what was just mentioned above, many people get comfortable in their ability to afford their new home because the bank has reviewed their income information and determined for them that they can. Your debt-to-income (DTI) ratio is what the bank calculates utilizing all of the documents that you provided, and there is a minimum acceptable ratio you need to meet on a monthly basis – generally 43%.

Here is how that works with an example using the numbers below:

➤ Monthly pre-tax income: $4,000 (assuming you make $48,000/year)

➤ DTI acceptable income: $1,720 ($4,000 x 43%)

➢ Monthly housing expense: $1,200 (mortgage, taxes, and insurance)

➢ Income left to pay other debt*: $480

From that $480, you now subtract every other payment that appears on your credit report (and this is where it can get misleading).

$480

-$220 car payment

-$40 credit card minimum payments

-$100 student loan payments

=$120 remaining

In this example, you would meet the DTI requirements because you still have money remaining after all of your debts are paid. Even if there was only $1 left, you would theoretically still get approved for the mortgage. This is where I want to caution you to look beyond just this calculation and take into consideration all of the other expenses you might have monthly that the bank never takes into consideration.

Look at the following example using some sample expenses that you will most likely have in addition:

-$4,000 monthly income

-$800 (payroll taxes, social security, and other deductions)

-$1,200 (monthly housing payment)

-$220 (car payment)

-$40 (credit card minimums)

-$100 (student loans)

-$200 (car insurance)

-$200 (utilities)

-$200 (transportation: gas, taxis, public transportation, tolls)

-$100 (cellphone)

-$100 (television and internet)

=$840 (money you have left after all of your "fixed expenses" are paid)

You might have just gone through those numbers and cannot understand why I am cautioning you. There is still $840 left, right? Or maybe, you went through those numbers and realized what was not taken into consideration. Where in that budget did you ever eat? There is no line item for groceries or the cost of eating out; whichever is your preferred method. I also didn't take into account having any type of social life. Those two items alone can wipe out the entire $840 and leave you no money to set aside in case of emergencies. For that reason, we will spend some time discussing budgets and why they are important next.

Adult Living Worksheet:

1) Identify how much money per month you can spend on housing:

2) How much cash do you have on hand to cover down payments, security deposits, etc?

3) What are the average rent prices in your current area or desired area?

4) Estimate the costs of the following expenses in your area:

-electric   -cable   -water

-gas   -garbage   -taxes

-insurance   -HOA fees   -parking

5) Create a folder containing the following documents so you are always prepared to take advantage of a rent/purchase opportunity:

-2 recent pay stubs

-2 years tax returns

-2 years W2s

"Money is a terrible master but an excellent servant."

-P. T. Barnum

Chapter 5: Money Management

Let's face it; some people are just better at managing money and paying bills than others. One can be great with numbers in general, but turn into a deer in headlights when there are dollar signs attached. Others, like myself, are terrible with numbers in general until they have a real world impact on their lives. And it does not get any more real than money. There is nothing free in the world and understanding how to control monthly finances is a crucial part of the equation in getting your money to work for you and saving money in unnecessary interest payments, penalties and late fees over time. So in this section we are going to cover the importance of creating a budget and adhering to it, best practices around emergency funds, and the basic principles of the banking industry.

Budgeting

Without an effective budget, you cannot take advantage of the Rule of 72, avoid bank fees, keep your credit score up to snuff, or a host of other adult responsibilities. And if you might be thinking, how can I budget when I hardly make any money, or I really don't have many bills right now, this section is especially important for you. Money management is a concept that many grown adults, with grown kids of their own in many instances, don't fully grasp and continue to perpetuate a self-fulfilling prophecy of financial hardship.

There are two main components to an effective budget – income and expenses. Those terms can also be known as credits and debits, ins and outs, positives and negatives – okay; I think you get the point. The more straightforward of the two is the expense side of the equation. Simply defined, expenses are the bills that you must pay. Generally, these are due monthly, like rent and phone bills, but there are some that you may need to pay quarterly or annually such as insurance premiums or property taxes. A number of examples were listed in the previous section regarding how much money you should spend on a monthly housing payment.

The easiest way to start putting a budget together is to sit down and draw a line down the center of a sheet of paper. First, list all of your bills on the left-hand side along with the monthly payment amount. This can be done by either taking it directly from the monthly bill you receive or dividing that quarterly bill by three or annual bill by twelve to arrive at the amount you should be putting away monthly. Trying to tackle these larger, less frequent expenses in one shot when they arise can wreak havoc on other obligations if you do not plan correctly. Many banks, Internet banks especially, will allow you to have multiple savings accounts without a service charge or minimum balance, and it is wise to have a separate account earmarked for each of these expenses so that money does not sit in your checking account, mingling with your daily living funds and lulling you into a false sense of security.

The trickier part of budgeting is figuring out how to manage the income column. The reason this can become complicated is due to the fact that not all employers pay with the same frequency. Some may pay you weekly, others every two weeks or twice a month, and others still once per month. Believe it or not, most of the options – even the once a month payment – can be easy enough to work with. If you get paid weekly, divide each monthly bill by four and put aside that much of your check each payday to cover it. If you get paid monthly, sit down right away and split the check to cover each bill. If you get paid twice a month (generally the 15th and 30th) split each expense in half and take out half from each check.

Maybe it's just me, but getting paid every other week has always made budgeting a struggle. Ten months out of the year, this pay frequency will still equate to getting paid twice. But there will be two months every year where you get an extra paycheck. Now, if you are fortunate enough to be able to cover all monthly bills from the two steady paychecks every month, this is actually simple. Just split each check to cover the bills as you would if you were paid on the 15th and 30th and those extra 2 paychecks per year can be saved or invested.

Now, if you can't cover the bills from those two checks every month, there are a few things you can do – in my opinion anyway. The first would be to not split those quarterly or annual bills I told you to split earlier, and just cover those from the extra two checks when they come in. The second is to make a chart or use the calendar on your phone to keep track of when all your bills are due and pay as close to the due date as possible to give you more wiggle room. Certain bills, like cable and phone bills, can actually be paid a few days late (not that I'm advocating that) without affecting your credit, incurring a fee or service interruption.

Another option I love to use, which combines earning rewards from the bank and getting your bills paid on time, is having all of these bills (as long as they do not charge a convenience fee to do so) set up to automatically charge to your credit card every month. Unlike auto debiting from your checking account or debit card, there is no risk of overdrawing your account and incurring unwanted fees with this method, and it reduces the number of payments you need to make – to ideally just one that pays your credit card off in full by the due date. And, as we will discuss shortly, credit cards give you free money, for up to a month in some cases. This can actually be a great responsible way to make sure all bills are paid on time while bridging the gap between your paychecks.

There is no right or wrong system to budgeting your money and paying bills so long as they are all paid on time. Experiment and see what works best for you. One last suggestion I have, though, that many people do not know exists, is the flexibility to pick and move some of your due dates around. Certain payments like your mortgage or rent will not be so flexible, (although it is a well-kept secret that you can make your mortgage payment that is always due on the 1st any time up to the 15th without incurring any penalties or negative credit reporting) but others will be. Most credit card companies will allow you to pick your exact due date; sometimes even let you change it once a year. If you buy or lease a car, inquire with the dealership if choosing your due date is an option – and it usually is. Since this will probably be one of your largest monthly payments outside of housing, it is usually prudent to pick a date in the middle of the month so that you don't find yourself forced to choose between paying for the roof or the wheels. In life, it never hurts to ask. The worst someone can say is no.

The example at the end of the previous chapter on mortgages is a great guide in case you want to do it the old school way – which I think is incredibly helpful to do a few times just to really get a feel for it, but there are also numerous apps available that can analyze your monthly spending by monitoring the credits and debits to your checking account.

Emergency Funds/Pay Yourself First

While I completely agree with the notion of paying yourself first, I also understand it can be anywhere from hard to downright impossible based on your financial situation. What it basically means is that you should include some type of savings strategy in your monthly budget. There are a number of reasons to want to save money. Vacations, gifts for birthdays and holidays, large purchases in the future and a host of others come to mind. But the one most people seem to overlook, or take the least seriously, is saving up an emergency fund. That just doesn't sound sexy at all, does it? Who wants to plan for an emergency? I can't answer that question, but what I can say for certain is that emergencies are going to happen. People lose jobs, cars break down, and medical issues not covered by insurance arise. Without proper planning, any one of these events can completely derail your life and the years you spend paying for it will be a bitter reminder of the emergency fund you didn't see the point in.

How much is a good amount to have an emergency fund? That is another great question that can vary wildly from person to person or situation to situation. The bare minimum any expert would suggest is to have at least three months of your expenses saved up. So whatever your budget numbers look like, take that total monthly expense column and multiply it by three. This gives you three full months to try and figure out the best way to resolve your financial hardship. I personally advocate for having six months of expenses saved, as some situations – like losing a job – are not resolved so quickly. There are others who would suggest twelve months, and there is nothing wrong with that either, it will just take you longer to reach that goal and you must remain patient and disciplined along the way.

Your vacation fund or discretionary savings account should never be confused with an emergency fund, either. Unless you are holding off on that trip until you're able to keep building the savings account first, the two should not be mingled. If there is money left every month in the budget after all the bills are paid, it is important to understand that this doesn't mean you should squander it on nights out partying and novelty purchases. In fact, we already spoke about how things like dining out, movies, etc., should already be built into your budget. Any extra money beyond that should be put away into some type of savings or investment vehicle so that the Rule of 72 gets to work for you. This ties in with two other powerful sayings, "work smarter not harder" and "have your money work for you." There are only so many hours in a week you can or want to work, so let your hard-earned money compound and earn you more.

Banking 101

One of the best things my parents ever did for me was insist that I get my own bank account when I first started working at the age of sixteen. Part of their motivation might have been to save the extra work of running to the bank to deposit my cash or check, then write out a check on my behalf every time I had a bill I needed to pay (yes at sixteen I paid my own bills – at least the luxuries like my video games, comic books and baseball cards). But knowing how they always tried to instill financial responsibility in me, I am sure that was the other motivating factor. Yet, even with the best of intentions, they never explained anything about bank accounts – merely took me to see the person they dealt with at the local savings bank and had them open me an account, where still nothing was explained about the mechanics of it all. So, over the next few years, and before I ever began working in the banking industry, I lived, learned and ultimately moved on to a bank that better suited my needs.

What needs should you consider when deciding on a bank? The answer to that question may range drastically based on your personal situation, but I will go ahead and share some of the non-negotiable things that a bank must have for me to even consider them. The first one is that they must not charge a monthly service fee, and I don't mean waiving the fee if you keep some ridiculous balance in your account. I understand they have a business to run so I don't mind meeting some kind of requirement, like establishing direct deposit, using a debit card or online banking – these things only make our lives easier anyway. The bank makes money by holding your money, off of debit card transactions wherever you swipe it, and in countless other ways. I do not need to pay them a monthly fee for the privilege of banking there on top of all of that.

The next non-negotiable can be a broad topic so I will elaborate, but at the heart of it, a bank needs to be convenient. A logical first thought for convenience is geographic branch locations. Do they have a physical presence where I live and/or work? In this day of electronic banking, there is hardly a need to make regular trips to the bank so it does not need to have a location right around the corner or even be the closest bank amongst the competition. I just like the peace of mind of knowing that, if I have an emergency where I need a large sum of cash, a cashier's check, or to speak with a person, that I am not limited to institutions that only have overseas call centers.

The other aspect of convenience that should be taken into account is the ease and reliability of the self-service options they offer. Online banking has become as integral to our daily routines as electricity, and quite honestly, some banks just do it better than others. If their system is down as much as it is working, and yes I have worked for banks where that is the sad truth of the matter, or if it takes as long to pay a bill online as it does to mail the check, it's kind of like the equivalent of buying a car that only makes left turns – it will get you where you want to go, as long as you expect to be late and frustrated when you arrive.

Relationship is the next important thing to consider, and I don't necessarily mean with the people who work there. I've worked and banked at dozens of institutions and can guarantee you, most bank employees do not stay in the same place for very long. By relationship, I mean having a range of products and services to meet all of your needs beyond just bank accounts. Can you get a car loan or a mortgage through the same bank? How about credit cards, bank checks or foreign currency? These are the things that many people do not think of upfront, usually not until there is a need for them, and then it is too late. At that point, you are left scrambling to find another bank that does offer those conveniences, and by the time all is said and done you may wind up running all over town to the three banks you now have just to accomplish what you could have done in one place if you did a little more research to begin with.

Now that we've covered all of the important factors to weigh when choosing where to bank, let's move on to your end of the bargain – keeping your account in good standing. You may have heard the expression, "balancing a checkbook," and while the term is a little dated since many people no longer use checks, the underlying premise is very much the same. While I've met some people throughout the years who would disagree with me here, this is not rocket science or high-level math. It is simply keeping track of how much money is in, or coming into, your account and how much you are spending. One area where almost all banks are the same is in the assessment of overdraft fees, which are charges that can cost you upwards of $40 per occurrence if your account goes negative (you spend more money than you have in the account).

In the old days, paper checks were the only option and there was a lag between when you mailed them out and when the funds were removed from your account. If you wrote a check on Monday for $100, and you had $150 in your bank account, that check may not get cashed until the end of the week or even the following week. So each day you check your account, it appears as if you never spent that money. If you withdraw $100 between Monday and when the check finally gets cashed, you will no longer have enough money to cover it and it will "bounce," or not be honored by the bank. It sounds basic, but when you have dozens of checks outstanding it can become easy to lose track of what your true balance is at any given point in time. While I could go through the mechanics of how to balance that checkbook, I don't think it is a relevant skill anymore. What I will advocate for, is that you become comfortable with paying bills online.

If you are like half the young people today, you may very well have parents who instilled the fear of God in you about banking online. But in all honesty, those concerns are as baseless as the other "old wives' tales" you were told as a kid. Doing your banking online does not make you any more susceptible to fraud or identity theft than living off the grid. In fact, I would argue that it helps you be safer. From the perspective of paying bills, the money is deducted from your account immediately so there is no need to guess what your balance is while waiting for checks to clear. Your balance is also updated in real-time, so any time you login you know exactly how much money is left in the account.

Having that kind of access at your fingertips will allow you to notice any suspicious activity as soon as it happens instead of waiting an entire month for your bank statement – when all of your money could already be drained from the account. Banks will reimburse you for any fraud against your account so long as you notify them within sixty days (for electronic fraud). If you are wasting thirty of those days waiting for a statement, you are at far greater risk than someone who catches it on day one. We live in an era where thieves are very good at what they do, and if they want to steal your money you do not have to be online to become a victim. I've witnessed elderly folks who don't even own a computer fall victim to online fraud and no one could explain how or why. The best prevention is being vigilant and not letting others scare you away from becoming comfortable with the way things will be done more and more in the future.

To stick with the current theme of banking, this is a good time to talk about one of life's great mysteries – the best way to pay for things. Depending on how technologically advanced you are, the best payment method may vary so I will start with the least favorable and we can work our way up from there. The absolute worst way to purchase something is with cash. There are a few exceptions to this rule, like if it is a small purchase, if the item will be discounted for cash, or if it's something illegal (no I won't give you any ideas here). Why is cash the worst option? First, it can be dangerous to carry it around. If you lose it or get robbed there is no way to replace it. Second, you have less recourse in the event that you are dissatisfied with a product or service as cash refunds are few and far between. There are numerous ways we will discuss next that are safer and quicker.

Slightly better than cash, yet another method I personally avoid at all costs, is using a debit card to buy things. It is only one notch up because at least the debit card can be replaced if lost, fraudulent transactions can be disputed, and it provides you some advantages in the event of a dispute with the vendor. My issue with debit cards is that they are virtually the same as paying with cash because the money is deducted from your checking account immediately. In the event that you return or dispute something, you are at the mercy of the merchant's timeframe to put the money back into your account. Imagine having $100 in your checking account and you are going away for the weekend. You go to put $10 worth of gas in your car and the attendant accidentally keys in $100. You catch it, they reverse it, and you're good to go, right?

Not quite.

In many instances, it can take 24 to 48 hours for that refund to process and the funds returned to your account, so you are now spending your weekend without money. The same thing can happen when you pay for gas at the pump or rent a car. A hold is typically placed on your debit card for more than the amount of the purchase as a way of the merchants protecting themselves. Think back to the part about balancing your checkbook and imagine what havoc could be wrought on your bill payments if excessive funds you do not have get frozen. I have a debit card for emergencies and only ever use it to take cash out of an ATM, preferably at my bank so as not to incur any additional fees.

Grow Up!

Here is where the list can diverge slightly so I will speak about the next two options being equally best and allow you to decide which one works better for you. The first is far more widely known and accepted but also gets a bad reputation, and based on the entire section we spent on interest rates it is understandable why that is many people's reactions to using credit cards. When used appropriately and responsibly though, credit cards cannot only be free money but also a way to get paid for your everyday spending through rewards programs.

In fact, that last part is so huge that I will not use any credit card that does not offer rewards. There are too many options out there to list so I will leave it up to you to conduct research on which one might make the most sense, but with a typical reward card it is not uncommon to rack up hundreds or thousands of dollars of cash back in a given year. I've done it personally and known many people, generally business owners, who spend far more money every month than I and have earned tens of thousands of dollars in rewards every year. These can be in the form of physical cash back, airline miles, gift cards or even credit toward payments on your monthly bill.

The next advantage of a credit card over the other options that we spoke about is that you are using the bank's money instead of your own. So all of those scenarios we mentioned about the debit cards, you never have the stress of waiting for your money to be refunded. There is generally no timeframe on when you need to file a dispute in order for the bank to honor it, which can be very helpful if you were not examining your statements closely and often enough. You also get the benefit of an interest-free loan on all of your purchases for up to a month, so long as you pay your credit card bill in full by the due date. There is a level of responsibility required to take advantage of this part though, so it might not be for everyone.

To eliminate that risk, you can treat your credit card like a debit card. By that, I mean make a payment as soon as you make a purchase so the money comes out of your bank account immediately and the credit card balance remains at zero. Most banks do not limit how many times a month you can make a payment on your credit card, another reason using online banking and electronic payments truly gives you the most control over your money. At the end of the day, add up every thing you purchased, login to your online banking account, and pay your credit card. Just like that you made your credit card a debit card.

The last option is your payment app of choice: Apple pay, Google pay, Samsung pay, etc. Before going into the benefits of these apps, it is important to note that they do require you linking them to a credit card or bank account, making the combination of the app and credit card a huge win-win. When your card is linked to the app you still receive all of the rewards you would have if you just swiped the card and will still be able to see all of your transactions on the credit card statement. The added benefit of using the app and not the physical card is that you are less susceptible to someone stealing your card information. You are also less likely to wind up in the awkward situation of finding out you left your wallet at home when you reach the cash register. I don't know about you, but I am more likely to leave the house without my pants than I am to forget my cellphone. Having that option is a safe and secure convenience I wouldn't want to live without.

Last topic on banking, I promise. I mentioned earlier choosing a bank that offers accounts with no monthly service fees because that is the easiest one to avoid. However, all banks have a host of other fees that they may charge for additional services, or as a penalty for being irresponsible. Knowing that many consumers are opting for choices without a monthly fee, banks have gotten more creative in the ways they are trying to make up this revenue and if you are not careful, you could unwittingly put that money in their pockets. I will offer you a list of some of the most common fees, but stress that you should be provided this information when you open your account, and if you're not you should not only ask for it, but possibly reconsider your choice to bank there at all as these disclosures are a federal regulation.

➢ Paper statement fee: Yep, there is a cost associated with printing and mailing statements and the most basic free accounts offered by some banks require you to get electronic statements to avoid this fee.

➢ Check order fee: Not only are they archaic and inefficient, as we discussed, but they are also no longer a luxury banks feel the need to provide for free. If you can secure your first order for free at account opening that should be all you need for a very long time.

➢ Check writing fee: Even after you paid for that book of checks you felt you needed to have, some banks limit the amount you can write every month without incurring additional fees.

➢ Overdraft fees: We covered this briefly before, but it is worth repeating. Thanks to some federal regulation this category is not as bad as it used to be, but in most instances you can still be penalized over $100 a day, depending how many times you overdraw your account. These fees are assessed per item and not per day. The most egregious example I can cite is a customer at my bank who was on a fixed income and averaged $500 per month in overdraft fees paid because of the excessive number of bounced items he had.

➢ Wire transfer fees: The cost associated with getting someone money immediately can be a nuisance, yes, but usually still more prudent than Western Union or MoneyGram.

➢ <u>Debit card replacement fees:</u> A complete scam in my opinion. The bank makes money every time you use it and should want to get a new one in your hand ASAP.

➢ <u>Cashier's checks and money orders:</u> Probably won't be a huge pain point unless you have a landlord who requires one every month, then it could run you over a $100 a year if not included for free with your checking account.

➢ <u>Teller usage fee:</u> Again, really? There's such a thing as a bank account that doesn't let you see a teller for free? The bank has to pay those tellers and is giving you a free account. Sometimes that trade-off is to train you not to need them at all.

Taxes

Benjamin Franklin has been quoted as saying, "In this world nothing can be certain but death and taxes." While it may sound unreasonable to put taxes in the same breath as something as permanent as death, after enough years in banking and dealing with the IRS it sometimes feels as if death would be the easier of the two to escape. Take a look around you. Our federal, state and local governments pay for just about everything we take for granted in our daily lives: the military, highways, and public transportation.

These entities are not charging for services or selling products to generate the money for all of these expenses, they are charging every person and company living and doing business in America taxes on the money they earn in order to provide these basic luxuries and necessities. Your social security number is linked to everything; every dollar your job pays you and each cent in interest your bank credits to your account.

This is not meant to sound negative because in all honesty, without taxes this country would collapse into chaos, but to prepare you for how the world works. Much like everything else in life, there are rules to playing the tax game and the more you know the less you are able to owe. A good accountant is an indispensable asset in life – right up there with a trustworthy mechanic and a doctor with good bedside manner. Please do not confuse the folks at the big name chain locations that spring up like weeds around tax time, or any of those tax preparation places you may see advertising the promises of getting you a "maximum refund" with a true accountant. While they may have one or two on staff very few, if any, of the folks working in these places are certified public accountants (CPAs). In fact, many may not even have college degrees and merely took a tax preparation course offered by the company they work for in order to become certified to do your taxes.

If you can't see how that might be concerning let's think for a moment about how the tax code in the United States might very well be the most complex set of rules in our society. Not only that, but there are numerous changes that go into effect every year based on legislation passed by our politicians. To say it is a full-time job staying abreast of what is new or no longer relevant would be a gross understatement. A CPA is someone who works in the field of accounting all year long and, for the most part, will be far better informed of these changes than a seasonal tax preparer. That guy or gal at your local tax shop probably only does taxes a few months out of the year and then goes back to waiting tables at Applebee's. Not that there is anything wrong with that, but I will leave their expertise to the menu specials of the day and not my income tax return. In case you are still not convinced, consider yourself warned that if one of these part-time tax preparers makes an error on your return and it triggers an audit, you are still personally responsible.

What is an audit you might be thinking? Oh, only the worst possible experience of your adult life is all. No, seriously, it might make prison or kidney stones seem like a trip to Disneyland. At least in a criminal trial, you are presumed innocent until proven guilty. At the outset of an audit you are basically guilty and must now prove to the auditor that you are innocent. The worst part about an audit is that it is not limited to the current year's tax return, they can and will review your last seven years of filings. If you can't provide a receipt or bank statement for something that happened that far back you could quickly find yourself on the hook for unpaid taxes or for paying back refunds they claim you were not entitled to.

Please, don't do it to yourself over the couple of dollars that could be saved. Would you choose a second rate doctor to perform open-heart surgery because they were 10% cheaper than a world-renowned surgeon? A good CPA will make sure you get the maximum refund or pay the least amount in taxes if you owe any, and do it all legally and knowledgeably. Many will represent you in the case of an audit. Yes, you are still responsible for any findings but it is a tremendous relief to have a professional act as the middleman providing all of the documentation the auditor requests. They can advise you on the retirement accounts and offer guidance on the flexible spending accounts offered by your company, both things we will speak about shortly. I would not trade my CPA for the world.

Money Management Tools:

1) Create an emergency fund plan. "In order to reach my goal of $_____ am going to start saving:

$_____ per week/month starting _____.

At the end of the year I will have $_____ and will need to do this consistently for _____ weeks/months (divide your savings goal by the timeframe).

2) Choose or reevaluate banking options by listing the three closest banks:

3) List three banks that have the best interest rates:

4) List three banks that have the best value in accounts (fees vs. services provided):

5) Open a new bank account for change banks based on the answers above. (Word of advice, never close your old back account until the new one is open for at least 3 months. This will allow for all of your debits and credits on the old account to switch to the new one).

"Choose a job you love, and you will never have to work a day in your life."

-Confucius

Chapter 6: Adult Thoughts on Work

No one wants to work for free, that goes without saying. But what is the best way to approach working when you first start out? That may sound like a stupid question, but the deeper you dive the more relevant it becomes. There is a difference between a job and a career; a distinction that not everyone will acknowledge or even realize exists. Generally speaking, a job is something that one does for a short period of time or to fill an immediate need, whereas a career is a path that you can follow for the rest of your life. Maybe you were a lifeguard or a babysitter over summer break and then went back to school. Those are jobs. But perhaps you took an internship at Google to learn about coding and web analytics because you are going to school for Computer Science. That would be the start of a career.

There are so many factors to consider when deciding what to do with your future that one of the biggest mistakes can quickly become using money as the basis for that decision. In this section, we are going to look at some of the decisions you will be faced with before picking a job or a career as well as one of the ways to set yourself up for success after you have a job offer from your employer of choice.

On or Off "The Books"

This topic is one of my personal favorites and something that I still find myself occasionally wrestling with. Working "on the books" means that you are officially an employee of the company you work for. As such, you receive a paycheck that has a number of items deducted from it, sometimes as high as 20% of your pay. So that $1,000 you made for the month only gives you $800 to take home. If you are thinking that sucks, have no fear we will come right back to that. "Off the books" is a scenario where you are not an actual employee of the company. Sure you show up, have a job to do, and get paid. But there is no record of your employment anywhere. The set amount of pay you agreed to is exactly what you get, so that entire $1,000 goes home with you. Doesn't sound like much of a decision, does it?

Let's talk about the negatives of working "off the books" since we already discussed the only positive thing I can think of – not to minimize keeping all of your money. First off, you have none of the protections that an "on the books" worker could be afforded, such as due process in getting fired, paid time off, or the option to enroll in medical benefits – if available. Secondly, this generally is not experience you can list on your resume. If a potential employer (landlord or mortgage company) wants to call and verify your employment, they would most likely be unable to, resulting in you looking deceptive for saying that you work there. Third, and to me the most important, is that you are not technically employed in the eyes of the federal and state government. So, yes you get to avoid paying income tax, but you are also forfeiting several other benefits you might not know you need until it is too late, which I will detail below in the benefits of working "on the books."

The first couple of benefits were spoken about as the disadvantages of working "off the books." Now, you are an official employee who can have work history verified, potentially qualify for medical benefits, and not have to worry about getting paid if you were sick and unable to come to work for a day or two. But the benefits run much deeper than that. Of that annoying chunk of money that gets withheld from your paycheck, the bulk of it goes to your federal and state income taxes – to pay for all those things we spoke about taking for granted earlier, but also something you can usually reclaim a portion of when you file your annual tax return. There are two smaller amounts deducted as well though that can prove to be lifesavers down the road.

One of these is unemployment insurance. I equate this to car insurance. You hope to never cash in on it, but should the need arise it can make all the difference in the world. As long as you've been consistently employed, each state varies on the exact time frame, and involuntarily lose your job, you will be able to collect a weekly paycheck from the state for a specified period of time in the form of unemployment benefits. It's important to note that I said involuntarily, such as a layoff or being fired situation, as you cannot collect simply because you quit.

The other small amount taken out every month is applied to Social Security benefits. The first thing many people think of when they hear Social Security is being old and retiring. While that is part of it, and an important one at that, it is not the only benefit. Social Security is also the agency responsible for making disability payments. So, if you were to get injured and unable to work, your payments into the Social Security fund would allow you to make a claim for benefits. When you are young and healthy it isn't always easy to look past the money you are losing for things that may never happen or seem like a lifetime away, but I assure you time flies. Getting in the habit of only working "off the books" can cause far more harm than good in the long run.

More to Work Than Salary

Much like it can be hard to wrap your head around the benefits of working for less money by choosing the "on the books" option, sometimes it can be easy to miss, or fail to understand, some of the more obscure benefits an employer may offer you beyond just the salary. I touch upon these in my other book, *"Seek & Employ,"* but want to make sure the benefits are understood. There are numerous perks a company can offer their employees that don't put money in your pocket now but can prove valuable to the employee and be more cost-effective for the employer than simply paying you a higher salary. In order to decide which offer is the better between two employers, it is important to understand exactly what they are and how they work – especially since none of them may seem that attractive when you first start acting like an adult.

One of the single biggest benefits you can hope to get is medical insurance, which oftentimes comes with a dental plan for a few extra dollars. If you are fortunate enough to still be covered by a parent's insurance then by all means don't rush into signing up for these, but if you aren't, this can be the difference between extra money in your pocket or paying off unforeseen medical bills for the rest of your life. At the time of writing this, obtaining your own health insurance outside of an employer-sponsored plan can set you back over $500 a month for a single person, whereas your employer plan could cost anywhere from half of that to possibly nothing at all. And whatever portion you do pay for that insurance is deducted from your paycheck before taxes are withheld so you are effectively paying even less.

The next unsung benefit is a company-sponsored retirement plan. Much like the Social Security conversation, it may be hard to factor in something that you won't see for forty years but there are more than enough reasons they should be taken seriously. Some of those plans, while increasingly rare in this day and age, do not require you to contribute anything and the employer puts away a percentage of your pay for you to start withdrawing when you hit retirement age. So, if you make $50,000 a year and they put 5% away, that's a free $2,500 a year, which effectively means your salary is actually $52,500.

The next plan that may be offered is a 401K, and the mechanics are a little more intricate – so bear with me. A 401K is employee-funded, oftentimes with the benefit of your employer matching what you contribute up to a certain dollar amount or percentage. Using the same $50,000 salary, let's say you decide to contribute 5% to your 401K plan. Approximately $210 will be deducted from your paycheck every month, once again before taxes are paid so effectively less than that, and put into an account with a number of investment options. This money cannot be touched until you reach the age of 59½, with certain exceptions, and grows tax-deferred allowing you to keep even more of your earnings. Now, let's pretend your employer is matching your contributions dollar for dollar. This means that they are also putting the same $210 a month away for you, essentially another free $2,500 per year. My advice is to find out the maximum amount your employer will match and put away at least that much money. Free money – even if you can't touch it right away – is still better than no money at all.

For the options of where to invest the money within your 401K, please speak to a financial adviser or company representative to understand the risk and rewards – I am solely focusing on the mechanics. If they do not have someone available to advise you, exercise some caution and get as much information as possible before making a decision. Legally, they must provide you with an overview of the options, called a prospectus, which will outline how well the individual options have done over time. This is not a foolproof method, but can be a very good barometer. In this prospectus you will see what rate of return (think back to our earlier talk about the Rule of 72) that the investment has averaged, generally shown over the last 1 year, 3 years, 5 years and 10 years. Those numbers will give you an idea not only of how well they have done, but also how much the account may fluctuate. And as a rule of thumb steer clear of investing a large percentage into the company's stock. In the event that they go out of business you have now lost both your job and retirement savings.

Flexible spending accounts are another great way to get more value from your job. There are a few different types of these accounts, but they all work on relatively the same principle. You pick a dollar amount or percentage of your paycheck to be withheld every month for certain purposes. As with a retirement account, these contributions are generally made pretax, so each dollar gets stretched further. But, unlike retirement accounts, these funds can generally be tapped into immediately as long as it is for qualified reasons. Some employers will also match contributions into these accounts, which is more free money. However, the benefit of being able to utilize the funds immediately can also be a double-edged sword. Typically, whatever you contribute to these accounts must be used in full by the end of the year or those funds can be forfeited. This is a situation where, my advice is to figure out how much money you will definitely use for each specific purpose by the end of the year and only put away that much, even if your employer will match more. Some of the most popular accounts of this type are:

➤ Health care savings account (HSA): As the name implies, the funds in this account can only be used to pay for qualified medical expenses. So, every trip to the doctor, prescription you fill, and over the counter drug or pharmacy-based purchase of most items (check your plan for specific requirements) can be paid for from this account. You are getting the tax benefit and planning in advance for expenses you probably would have incurred anyway, how can you lose?

➤ Dependent savings accounts: Sometimes it can be difficult to work if you have young children or elderly parents who require you to care for them. The costs of childcare in this country are absurd, to the point where sometimes it feels like you are paying just to have a job. Home health care is not too far behind that in terms of cost, either. Knowing that you will need to spend this money anyway, why not take advantage of paying before taxes and possibly getting some money out of your employer toward the cause? This can easily equate to an extra couple hundred dollars a year that you make/save.

> ➤ <u>Transportation spending accounts:</u> Also referred to as "commuter plans," these are directly tied to what it costs you to travel to and from work. The expenses typically covered by these accounts include bus tickets, train tickets, carpool/rideshare expenses, and parking expenses for your personal vehicle. Unfortunately, gas and mileage are almost never reimbursable, but if you live in a major city like New York or Los Angeles, the other costs of commuting are generally the most cumbersome. This is yet another category where you are making/saving money simply by planning and taking advantage of your employer's offerings.

Assuming that you take advantage of all of these spending accounts as well as the retirement plan and that your employer matches something on any of them, the same $50,000 yearly salary could effectively be more like $55,000 to $60,000. Much like the fine print in buying a car or paying off a credit card, understanding the value of your benefits package can make a significant financial impact on your life both now and in the future.

Negotiating a Raise

Even if you have yet to begin working, it is always helpful to understand the often convoluted mechanics of how to get a pay raise or promotion over the course of your career. Because the criteria will range widely from company to company, and industry to industry, this is not meant to be specific to any one situation, but there are some general best practices you can employ almost anywhere to help you understand the process and paint yourself in the best possible light.

One of the key ways to set yourself up for success is by asking this very question on your initial interview. It may sound a bit forward to inquire about promotions before you have been hired, but I assure you it will speak volumes to your character. As a hiring manager, I always sought out candidates who were interested in career advancement because that usually meant they were not just showing up for a paycheck and had a genuine interest in going above and beyond. Asking the question will not guarantee you a promotion or even getting hired, but it most certainly will not hurt your chances, either. It will also give you a reference point to circle back to with your manager when the time may arise for you to ask for that raise or apply for a promotion.

Whether you asked the question at the interview stage or not, it is also advisable to have periodic performance check-ins with your manager. Many companies have structured midyear and end of year review processes where your overall performance will be formally evaluated and possibly given a rating. These are great tools for you to use and should not be looked upon as a way for your employer to sandbag you – yes it does happen, but if you are doing your job well and know what is expected of you, then there should be no issues.

This brings me to my next point about not waiting six months for one of these opportunities to arise only to find out that you and your boss are on different pages, or worse, reading different books. Work throughout the year to set regular check-ins with your direct supervisors where you have informal conversations about how your performance stacks up, discussing what you were doing well and areas you can improve on. Send a thank-you email to your supervisors after the discussion and summarize your takeaways so that there is a written record of it should any confusion arise later. Then, don't only take those suggestions and implement them, but find a way to track your progress against those items, either quantitatively or qualitatively, so that you can compare your version of progress with theirs.

Grow Up!

<u>Employment Thoughts Worksheet</u>

1) What are your initial thoughts regarding working on the books vs. off the books?

2) Identify the top job opportunity you might have in each category and compare the positives and negatives:

3) To evaluate different job offers, identify which of the following benefits are offered and any potential employer matches:

-Health Insurance   -Dental Insurance   -Vacation

-Pension   -Health savings account   -401k

-Dependent savings account   -Commuter savings account

"There are worse things in life than death. Have you ever spent an evening with an insurance salesman?"

-Woody Allen

Chapter 7: Insurance

It seems like every day the insurance industry creates new products and gimmicks to separate people from their money, and that is impressive because they have been swindling people for over a century. Generally speaking, the only profession that evokes as negative a connotation as that of used car salesman is an insurance salesman – specifically life insurance. All insurance serves a purpose, but that doesn't mean all insurance is created equally or priced the same. For the purpose of focusing on the ones that will be the most relevant starting out in life, we will only look at life, health and auto insurance. and stick to the basics as this is another topic that could have an entire book dedicated to it.

Automobile Insurance

Depending upon where you live, car insurance will be a mandatory expense in order to own a vehicle. In fact, there are only three states that do not require it, so if you happen to live in one, either be thankful you don't need it or pray that you are never in an accident with someone who chose not to get it. There are levels of insurance that dictate what your insurance company will pay out for in the event of a claim, and each one has specific maximums they will pay up to.

> Liability: This is the no-frills car insurance that will probably give you no benefit other than meeting your state's requirement. With a basic liability policy, you are not covered for any damage to your vehicle under almost all circumstances. This coverage strictly exists to protect other people you may cause injury or damage to in the event of an accident.

> Collision: The title is self-explanatory on this one – sort of. This level of coverage includes the basic liability, but will also cover you for any damage your vehicle may suffer. That damage, however, must be the result of some kind of car accident. It generally will not cover things other than your car crashing into another car, building or object. Falling trees, golf ball-sized hail, or surging floodwaters that bring a boat crashing into your driveway will most likely not be covered.

> Comprehensive: This is the gold standard in car insurance. This will cover the basics of liability and collision, but also against those more obscure accidents mentioned above. Also, if your car gets stolen you will most likely be covered for the replacement value (cost of buying a comparable vehicle).

Now just because one level of insurance covers everything and another covers hardly anything does not mean it is a clear-cut choice. There will be significant price differences in the levels of coverage, so having more insurance than you need could be just as costly as being underinsured. If you own a brand new BMW, you can probably justify paying extra to make sure that it is covered in every way possible. On the other hand, if you are driving a ten-year-old car with 200,000 miles, you will most likely not see a huge benefit in having the higher, more expensive level of coverage. Hopefully, your insurance agent is honest and guides you in the right direction, but at least you have the basic knowledge to understand what they try to delve deeper into.

Life insurance

This has evolved so much over the years I can't even accurately tell you how many "variations" there currently are, and that is scary considering I was a licensed life insurance agent for over ten years. So, for the sake of this overview, we will look at the two main categories most of the newfangled creations fall into. But before we go any further, let me try and save you some money. If you are single, without kids, and don't own a home – you do not need to waste your money on life insurance.

Much like car insurance, you don't buy life insurance in the hopes of cashing in on it, because in this case, that means you are dead and someone else gets the money. A more appropriate term for life insurance is "income replacement insurance" since that is what it is designed to do – allow for your loved ones to carry on with the household expenses after the loss of your income. Agents will try to sell you on the fact that the younger you are when you buy it, the cheaper it is – and that is absolutely true. Insurance premiums increase with age. But what good is paying a lower amount now when you are throwing money out the window in the long run? And that's just the first trap of the timeless life insurance juggernaut. The debate of term insurance versus whole life can give even the savviest individual a migraine and buyer's remorse, but I will do my best to explain the difference.

➢   <u>Term insurance:</u> Think of it exactly like your car insurance. You pick a specific period of time, usually between ten and thirty years, then pay a set monthly premium for that entire time period. If you happen to die, your beneficiaries get paid. If you don't, your insurance ends and you can either renew for another term of your choosing or walk away. The new rates will be much higher than what you were previously paying as they are based on your new age, but you also probably don't – or at least shouldn't – need anywhere near as much coverage, as at this point hopefully your kids will be older and the house closer to being paid off.

➢   <u>Whole Life:</u> This is an insurance product that is sold with so many different descriptions and names that it's hard to keep up with. The most important thing to remember when it comes to whole life, cash value, universal life, variable life, or whatever other name insurance companies come up with for it next, is that you do not need it. Unless, of course, you are a trust fund baby or self-made millionaire at a young age, otherwise the added costs far outweigh any of the potential benefits they may try to sell you on. I also advise getting a book on basic finance concepts if you want to research the topic in more depth, and caution strictly taking the word of your insurance agent or financial adviser without educating yourself first, as they typically make triple the commissions to sell you one of these products over the more cost-effective term insurance.

Now that I've given you my cautions and advice I will give a very quick overview of why this does not usually make sense for most people.

➢ Almost no one needs insurance for his or her entire life. That's like having car insurance and no car to drive. Remember the term, "income replacement." When you are retired, and all of your major expenses are paid off, there is no need left to insure – no income left to replace.

➢ It costs exponentially more than term insurance for a lot of benefits that are really just smoke and mirrors.

➢ It is sold as having a cash value account that you can tap into in case of an emergency. They do not tell you that this "cash value" account is really just a portion of the money you overpaid for the policy to begin with, and if you do take the money out of here it will be considered a loan that they will charge you interest on. That's right, paying interest on your own money.

> Your policy can self-destruct for any number of reasons without you being aware of it. So, let's say you forget to make your loan payments on your own money you borrowed. The insurance company will usually deduct them from whatever is left in the cash-value account, if anything. If the cash value drops to zero, your policy will lapse. Now, if you still need insurance, you will have to buy a new policy at higher premiums based on your age at that time.

Health Insurance

This topic cannot be summed up in one section. It probably can't be done justice in a whole book. Heck, the Affordable Care Act was passed through Congress at 2,300 pages long and an additional 16,000 pages have been added to it in the seven years since it was enacted. It is conceivable that not a single person in the Senate or House of Representatives read more than the cover page. Health care in this country has always been a complex topic and this just made it far more difficult. To put that in context, I held a New York State Accident & Health insurance license for many years, which means I passed the state test and was qualified to sell it to the general public, yet I still struggle to make heads or tails of some wording. But with that said, I will do my best to simplify as much of the complexity that you are bound to encounter so that at least the terms are somewhat familiar.

The first thing to know is that not everyone has health insurance nor is it required in order to be treated in the event of an emergency. And no, that's not extreme. That is about the only time you cannot be refused medical attention. If you have a cold and want to go to see a regular doctor most will not see you without insurance unless you pay in cash upfront. Some doctors go so far as to not even see cash-paying patients at all. This means you will most likely wind up waiting and hoping it goes away with Nyquil and other over-the-counter medications. But when it doesn't, and turns into pneumonia or something else potentially life-threatening, and you show up at the emergency room they are now obligated to treat you. The part no one explains or thinks about though is that just because you are entitled to *care*, that in no way shape or form means you are entitled to *quality care*. Knowing you don't have insurance means the hospital will be hard-pressed to admit you, even if that is the better option, because chances are you will not be able to pay the bill for the stay, which is probably a good assumption as it can run into the tens of thousands of dollars for a few nights.

That last part was not meant to scare you into buying insurance, just to make you aware of the way the medical world works when we don't have any. In all honesty, it does not become a whole lot better if you do have insurance, although, it can at least be more predictable. But this does not translate to cheap by any means. If you are fortunate enough to get a job that offers benefits like medical insurance you will be able to take advantage of group discounts and get a policy (for a single person) for around $200 a month, which as we spoke about in pre-tax payroll deductions, effectively costs you even less. Should you need to get insurance on your own, expect to spend more in the area of $500 per month.

In either instance, the amount you pay for insurance is only the beginning, unless of course you never get sick or go to visit the doctor. Most plans these days will allow you to go visit a doctor for regularly scheduled wellness visits such as an annual physical for free, but any other reason will bring about a charge in the form of a "deductible." Beyond the cost of the visit, you may incur more expenses in the form of "coinsurance" payments if special tests or exams like MRIs or CAT scans are needed. If prescription medication is needed there is a good chance you will have to pay for that as well, but at a discount to what the general public would pay. We are going to speak about all of those terms in more detail shortly but first I want to make you aware of the different plans and how to pay attention to the most important parts of your specific plan overview.

Most plans have two options when you enroll: a "high deductible" and "low deductible" plan and they mean exactly what the name implies. If you opt for a low deductible plan, the bill will be lower each time you go to a doctor but in turn, you will pay more for it each month. With a high deductible plan, your out of pocket cost will be higher for each doctor visit but your monthly premiums will be far lower. Many people get caught up on this choice and no one ever seems to know which way to go. I may be the only person on Earth who sat down to do the math on my own plan options and as such can honestly say, in a worst-case scenario, they will both wind up costing you the exact same, the only difference being when the money comes out of your pocket. However, if you are relatively young and healthy, I have always opted for the lower monthly premium and higher deductible knowing that I would hardly go to the doctor.

Your plan overview will outline A LOT of important information that doesn't usually make much sense. The two most important numbers to pay attention to, after the cost of the plan itself, are deductible limits and coinsurance limits. These numbers may range from $1,500 to $7,500 each and in any given year there is a possibility that you may have to come out of pocket for all of both. Below those items is a very long list of different medical terms and procedures with the associated percentages that your insurance will cover. Those percentages will also be listed in two separate columns and vary whether the doctor you go to is considered "in-network" or "out-of-network." In-network means that your doctor accepts your specific type of insurance and therefore you will pay a smaller percentage to visit them whereas an out-of-network doctor is not a preferred provider of your insurance and you will pay a higher percentage. For this reason, it is always advisable to check as to whether your current doctor is in-network or not before choosing a particular plan, and if you don't have a regular doctor you visit try to choose one that is in-network.

As promised, some clarification on terms and illustrations:

➢ Deductible – Also called co-payment, is the flat amount of money you will pay out of pocket each time you see a particular doctor. It can range from $25 for your primary care doctor to $50 or $100 for a specialist, or $250 or more for an emergency room visit. The only time this payment goes away is when you hit your deductible limit for the year. Let's say that maximum amount is $2,500 and each individual visit costs you $25. You would need to go 100 times before your next visit did not charge you a deductible.

➢ Coinsurance – The variable amount of money you must pay for additional medical-related expenses after your initial visit. These amounts are determined by the chart in your plan overview that tells you what percentage insurance will cover. This number is variable because the costs of medical services vary widely. If your insurance covers 80% of a procedure that is

$1,000 you are responsible for paying $200. If it is $10,000 then you are paying $2,000. Once you have reached your plan's coinsurance maximum though, you will not have to pay this anymore, at least not for the current calendar year.

➢ Prescription drugs – Some plans will cover generic drugs more so than name brands. It is important to know this because today almost all name-brand drugs are available in generic options. It all depends how your doctor writes your prescription so mentioning to them that you prefer the generic cannot hurt and they will almost always oblige. **(See Appendix 7-1)**

Insurance Check-up Activity:

1) Do you have the right automobile insurance? Call your agent and ask for prices on each. Is the price difference worth the benefit for your situation?

    -Liability:

    -Collision:

    -Comprehensive:

2) If you don't own a home, have kids or anyone relying on your income, then you do not need life insurance. But if you do, calculate how much coverage you need by using the guide below and adding the totals together.

    *Mortgage balance

    +Annual income x 6

    +Total outstanding debt

    +Estimated tuition needs

    =Approximately how much insurance you need

3) Perform a health insurance check-up if you are currently covered, or use the template below to help shop plans:

    (A) Annual premium amount

    (B) Deductible limit

    (C) Coinsurance maximum

    (A+B+C) Total possible cost per year

"Successful people aren't born that way. They become successful by establishing the habit of doing things unsuccessful people don't like to do."

-**William Makepeace Thackeray**

Chapter 8: Grown-up Habits

The word "habit" usually has a very negative connotation associated with it. Our brains are wired to jump to all of the different bad habits one can have, like smoking, drinking, even the biting of fingernails and other nervous tendencies. And while there is truth to that interpretation, there is an entire other side to habits that often gets overlooked. Good habits may require more focus and determination to build than their detrimental counterparts since the activities involved may not be as enjoyable or feel as rewarding in the moment, but they will also help set you on the path for success. Any of the habits that will be discussed can wind up classified as good or bad depending on what you choose to make of them.

Based on research performed by people smarter than myself, it is estimated that it takes about two months – yes sixty days – to form a new habit. That means consistently performing the activity in question in some way, shape or form every single day during that period. Conversely, this can also be how long it takes you to break a bad habit. Knowing the amount of time involved should be more optimistic than discouraging, though. If you are struggling to wake up earlier or get to the gym consistently, and have only been at it for a week or two, it should be comforting to know that you just need to keep working at it a while longer. But that is also a long period of time to quit doing something that is negatively impacting your productivity and all the more reason not to form bad habits.

Technology Addiction

This topic is incredibly painful to write about, admit that I have myself at times, and to date myself on how far technology has come in the last three decades. When I was growing up, cellphones did not become an affordable mainstream luxury until college and even then devices had a fraction of the functionality they do now with service plans that were far more expensive. We relied heavily on beepers and payphones (if you're not sure what either look like, Google them – probably the only way you will come across either in 2019). Game consoles started out at Atari and advanced through the ranks to what we have today, making my generation far more appreciative of everything technology has provided. But because of the speed at which things have advanced, the younger generations do not realize just how good they have it and tend to take everything for granted.

A few years back I wrote a blog based on a skit by the comedian Louis CK on how technology is killing communication skills. The skit was called "Generation of Spoiled Idiots" and looking back on it, while I still believe everything I wrote to be true, I feel like I left out so much more than just the effect on communication. Before you get offended by the label of "stupid idiots" remember it is a comedy piece and it could be better interpreted as "impatient and ungrateful." That might not sound much better, but let's look at the reality for a moment. Twenty years ago you could only get Internet if you were hardwired into a phone line and fortunate enough that the servers were not too overloaded for you to be able to connect. We've since moved to Wi-Fi, mobile data and even mobile Wi-Fi. You can even connect while on a cruise ship or airplane. Amazing, right?

But what's the first thing that happens to many people when this new luxury isn't working for some reason? Let's say the Wi-Fi on your airplane is out, or your mobile carrier's network is lagging due to reception issues. It becomes an instant temper tantrum and we want to lash out at somebody as if one of our Constitutional rights were just infringed upon. In fact, some would probably give up one or two of those civil liberties before parting with the ability to stay connected. But why? How necessary is it really to be plugged into your network every waking, and sometimes sleeping, hour of the day? And since it has become a struggle even to the older generation that has now become very reliant on technology for our jobs and families, I know from first-hand experience working with young people, it is so much harder for those who have basically had a smartphone in their hand since they were in diapers.

Just for context so this does not come across as my opinion instead of the fact that it is, many companies are starting to recognize just how detrimental to our mental health an over stimulus of technology can be. When e-mail first became available on mobile devices many employers flocked to the idea of having their employees either receive work email on personal devices or provide company-issued phones so that work could be addressed after hours. This effectively meant that when you went home for the day and were no longer getting paid, your boss still had a way of reaching you and *stealing* your time. Sure, you didn't have to answer, but if all of your coworkers were, there was the fear it would look bad on you. Fast forward a decade or so and many employers have completely reversed course on this. Part of the reason stems from people suing them for this abuse of their personal time, but another part is from the realization that this extra productivity was causing more harm than good and actually proving to be counter-productive.

Being too connected, not just to your phone but any form of digital technology: social media, email, Skype, etc., can cause severe damage to a number of our basic human emotions. Once those feelings become unbalanced it can be incredibly difficult to restore equilibrium, and worse, can lead to withdrawal symptoms far worse than those of a recovering alcoholic or drug addict. No, that is not an exaggeration.

Imagine for a moment what would go through your head if you had two important emails to respond to, a few unanswered text messages and a phone call scheduled in the next hour. Suddenly, your phone dies – not the battery but just stops working for no reason. You are nowhere near a computer and all of the cellphone stores are closed. Do you feel it? That sense of anxiety creeping in as you start to think about what the other people waiting for your responses are going to think. That anxiety can quickly turn into panic and before you know it you are running around like a lunatic trying to borrow a phone and hope you remember the phone numbers and email addresses from your contact list.

I've been there; the feeling is real. Beyond just that extreme example, it is all too common for fear, anxiety, stress, and depression to creep into our minds because of the importance we have assigned to our social media personas or virtual worlds. There are people who literally cannot tell the difference between getting approval from Instagram followers they have never met and their childhood best friends. Life is not a virtual popularity contest; it is about forming and fostering real-life connections that will help you throughout the years. Life is not about creating online civilizations or growing your farm, it should be about building your personal brand and growing something tangible that will help yourself, your family and humanity down the road.

Once you are able to disconnect from this fake world and fake friends, you will have much more clarity on what really matters. Because of this addiction to technology and social media, Millennials tend to be far more disconnected from reality and devoid of emotions than any other generation. Human interactions are lost in favor of virtual ones, people are viewed as nothing more than a milestone follower, avatar or screen name. This happens to be a period in time where we as a society have experienced more mass shootings and murders by juveniles than I can ever remember.

I'm not qualified to say there is a direct correlation, but considering the current content of video games on the market that are played for mind-numbing lengths of time on end, the insane things that are posted on blogs and social media sites and streamed on the Internet, that should be reason enough to give us pause. We shouldn't believe everything we read or hear, especially from those who are grossly unqualified to speak about it (but alas social media has given every moron a platform) and disconnecting from time to time is the best way to hit the internal reset button in our minds and stay true to our humanity while resisting the lures of virtual acceptance and false existence.

Cooking vs. Eating Out

Cooking was once a crucial life skill that was taught in high school. Yes, it was called "Home Economics" and in retrospect was probably a bit sexist in nature. But the importance of that skill goes far beyond who should be in charge of cooking in the household and looked at more as something everyone should be able to do. The transition from a college dorm room where gourmet cooking might have consisted of Raman noodles and boxed Mac N' Cheese to a kitchen of your own where the sky is the culinary limit can be daunting. Going from a campus dining hall or meal plan where prices ranged from cheap to free to real-world eateries can also be a shock to the budget when you are first starting out. But there are two very important reasons one should try to find a happy balance between the meals you cook at home with when and where you eat out.

Let's talk price first since that is usually what gets more people's attention than the less obvious, longer-term health benefits. Learning how to cook can and will save you a tremendous amount of money over the course of each week, month and year. Even if you are a very slow learner and have difficulty with boiling water, there are meals you can make that don't involve the stove. Getting comfortable with the supermarket and art of grocery shopping is half the battle. You can buy a sandwich at your local deli for around $5 – $8 and have lunch for one day, or you can buy a loaf of bread and cold cuts at the supermarket for about $10 to have lunch for the entire week. A steak dinner out at a nice restaurant will run you between $20 – $50, but a trip to the grocery store can whip up the same thing for about $15 with plenty of food to save for another night. Those examples run the extreme of cheap lunch to expensive dinner, but that is just the foundation of the concept.

For illustrative purposes, let's assume that you actually eat three meals a day. If you intend to eat every one of those out in some fashion or another the monthly price tag might scare you into thinking twice. Even if you only spent $5 per meal, (a feat that really isn't even feasible at McDonald's these days unless you order individual items off the dollar menu) that still comes out to $15 a day. That is $450 per month spent on the same nutritionally dubious food day in and day out, or $5,400 per year. Next time you are in McDonald's, which hopefully isn't often, take a look at the menu prices and you will see that chances are you will be paying more than $5 per meal on average. And if you live in certain larger cities, like New York, you can oftentimes find yourself spending $15 on a single meal as opposed to the entire day. The money starts to add up quickly.

The next reason to strongly consider learning to cook, or at least to shop and prepare some simple meals at home, is the health factor mentioned earlier. I know that when we are younger it is not usually a concern to look at the nutritional information (calorie count, fat, cholesterol, etc.) for what goes into our bodies. The younger we are the faster our bodies seem to metabolize food and the less of the negative effects are felt. But as the body gets older, the years of poor nutrition and mistreatment begin to take a toll that can cause all kinds of health issues. Fast food is almost all processed and loaded with enough sodium to cause instant heart attacks. If something is too good to be true, it probably is. That is exactly why any hamburger – cooked, packaged and ready to order – that costs a dollar should probably make you think twice.

Even if you decide to get in the habit of checking nutritional information as a way to justify continuing to eat out, that becomes a very slippery slope. Not all fast food chains advertise their nutritional information, although in some places it is mandatory that they do so. You can estimate by comparing to similar items on other chain restaurant menus but that is more work than it is productive. Even the seemingly healthy options like a grilled chicken sandwich or salad can wind up weighing in at over 1,000 calories thanks to all of the *extras* such as dressing and sauces that get piled on. If you think the local neighborhood deli or diner is a healthier option, don't be so quick to assume. At least the big chains are somewhat required to disclose nutritional information but those little mom and pop stores are not. The chef in the back could be scrambling your eggs in a vat of butter or the deli clerk slathering enough mayonnaise on the roll to clog an artery. The best way to ensure that you are eating healthy is by sourcing it and cooking it yourself.

So maybe you are convinced you should take more charge of your meal plan but have no idea where to begin. That evil technology we spoke about, when used appropriately, can actually solve many of those issues for you. There are countless websites dedicated to sharing free recipes complete with step-by-step instructions on how to prepare the food, many will even let you build a virtual shopping cart so that you are sure not to miss any ingredients on the trip to the supermarket. You can watch YouTube videos of people making certain meals. There is an entire TV channel dedicated to cooking shows, even virtual cooking classes if time is a challenge to attend a physical one. There really is no excuse not to learn the basics.

There is a modern convenience now available that can help you out as well if the whole concept of deciding what to make, shopping, then cooking is just too daunting. Meal kits have grown increasingly popular over the last few years, now with numerous options to choose from. These kits will have everything you need (minus some basic staples like milk and butter that should always be in your refrigerator anyway) shipped right to your door – recipe cards with instructions and ingredients. I have tried a few different ones with varying degrees of satisfaction in terms of price and variety, but all in all, they can serve a purpose.

Some are more cost-effective than others but ultimately they are all still more expensive than shopping yourself, yet cheaper than eating out. The real reason I mention them here is because they almost all offer a new customer discount making them reasonably priced for the first few orders. This allows you time to practice cooking and, if you like what you make, to keep the recipe card and make it yourself at a future date after canceling the membership. Don't be afraid to try a few different companies to take advantage of the specials and stockpile some recipes while honing your skills.

Time Management

This is one of the most prominent characteristics of the super-wealthy and productive, and one that is much more difficult than it seems. When first out of school it can be difficult to start juggling all of the added tasks and events of life. In college, you were probably able to set your own class schedule and did so in the best way to fit your lifestyle. Some of your only responsibilities consisted of making it to class on time, studying, eating, and perhaps doing laundry. That relaxation and predictability can all get turned upside down as soon as you land your first job.

In the real world, you do not get to set your work schedule unless you are self-employed. Your company will either have standard office hours or set workweek, or your manager will provide you with a schedule each week that changes based on the need of the business. If that means working late on a Friday, it won't matter if that's your trivia night, you will be in the office or heading to the unemployment line. Commuting to and from work will likely take up far more of your time than walking from the dorms to classrooms did and that leaves fewer hours in the day for the rest of the chores you will need to address. Those may just be the basics of grocery shopping, going to the laundromat and cooking but don't be fooled – the time starts to add up quickly. And that's all before you schedule anything *fun*.

There was a keyword in that last sentence; actually, it was

used three times because it is so important. That word is *schedule*. Schedule can be thrown around commonly when discussing plans for the day or week, but without any way of tracking and implementing it becomes nothing more than a wish list. You can either control your time or your time will control you. I started out by mentioning how time management is a strong point of most successful people and that is because they are in total control of their days. There are many top executives who wear the same exact outfit every single day (not the same clothes from the day before but a weekly wardrobe that is all identical). Why do they do this? To avoid wasting any time in the morning on decisions that are not going to be impactful. Sure, deciding what to wear probably only takes a few minutes at most and this example may seem a bit extreme, but when you are working sixteen-hour days and cramming them full of meetings and calls, that time is money. I'm not suggesting everyone needs to do this, simply pointing out the lengths some will go to in order to be masters of their schedule.

The first thing that you should put in place if there is to be any hope of time management is a calendar of some kind. There is no hard-and-fast rule on what kind of calendar: an app linked to your phone or email, pinned up on your wall, a blotter on your desk, a daytimer or in your briefcase. Despite my earlier gripes on technology, I do still prefer the digital option – but not because I want to stare at it all day long. Apps have the ability to send you reminders, which may very well be more important than even entering the item into the calendar in the first place. As the day gets busy, taking the time to look through a physical calendar or even remembering to try to do that becomes very unrealistic. That annoying ding from your phone can be a lifesaver. On more than one occasion I've been reminded of an important phone call a few minutes prior and was able to scramble quickly enough to catch it thanks to having my app up to date.

There are a few nuances to the calendar alerts to make them the most effective though. Most calendars default to set a reminder for five minutes prior to the event. Now, in many circumstances that probably isn't a whole lot of time to make a difference. If the task in question is for a phone call appointment, sending an email, or simply following up on something it will probably be just fine. When the event is for a physical appointment or meeting that is somewhere other than the location you normally are on that given day then a reminder for the day before will be a better option so the necessary preparations can be made in advance. For events that occur infrequently and are larger in scale – like a business trip, vacation, or large gathering that was scheduled far in advance – a reminder of anywhere from a week to a month in advance can save you a whole lot of stress later on by not leaving you down to the wire with no time to prepare.

Like everything else covered in this book, there is no right or wrong way to implement the suggestions. The only wrong way would be to do nothing at all. It is good to get in the habit of using a calendar early on in life and plugging everything into it. Schedule your meal breaks, nights out with friends, even the trip to the grocery store. Nothing in life is fixed and there will be times our schedule doesn't work out as planned. That is OK and completely normal. But knowing in the moment that something is not going to work out affords you the ability to proactively reschedule it on your terms instead of realizing after the fact that you forgot and are now subjected to any repercussions that go along with that lapse.

<u>Grown-up Reflections:</u>

1) Identify how many hours per day you spend on the each of the following technology sites and then create a schedule to limit that time to no more than an hour a day (combined for all):

    -Facebook

    -Twitter

    -Instagram

    -Other

2) Identify your three favorite meals, then find easy recipes online to start making them yourself. Practice makes perfect!

3) Sign up with a meal kit company and analyze the benefit:

    -<u>Company</u>   -<u>Price</u>   -<u>Easy</u>   -<u>Quality</u>   -<u>Satisfied</u>

4) Identify two methods you will adopt to manage a calendar so that you control your time and your time does not control you:

"A good plan today is better than a perfect plan tomorrow."

-George S. Patton

Chapter 9: Planning For The Future

When we are young, there are a whole lot of things that we either never want to think about or don't even realize are potential topics of conversation. That is exactly why I placed this chapter after the one on habits. Look, no one wants to think about growing old and dying. As kids, the prospects of getting a driver license and being able to walk into a bar and drink legally are so glamorous that we cannot wait to grow up. But once you hit twenty-one, and age no longer restricts you from access to anything except for AARP or reduced car insurance premiums, there doesn't seem to be such a desire to think about where we may be in the future.

I can't lie or sugarcoat it. Getting old is no fun. But the alternative is far less appealing. And yes, unless you are immortal or have found the fountain of youth, that option is death. Since we can't fight growing old, the least we can do is plan accordingly so that our golden years are just that – golden. A failure to plan when you are younger can lead to living on a fixed budget of whatever Social Security, if it is even still around, provides you. Throughout my banking career I have watched too many senior citizens come in toward the end of the month to hope their check was deposited earlier than expected because they were flat broke. Or worse, take on part-time jobs to bridge that gap.

Tomorrow isn't promised to anyone, but the odds are in your

favor. Think carefully about what you want to do for the rest of your life and do not just blindly do what all of your friends and family members suggest. They will not be the ones eating canned soup with you at seventy, so own your future while you still have some input.

Self-Employment Pitfalls

This section is for the budding entrepreneurs out there. The world of self-employment can be free from many of the intricacies of the corporate world but it does come with a host of other challenges, some of which can really set you up for failure if not prepared. One of the best things about being self-employed is that you can control your paycheck. So long as your business or idea is profitable, it stands to reason that the harder you work or the more time you invest in it the more money you will see in return. Some months you may draw more in salary than others, some months maybe you don't draw any at all. But just because your income does not come in the form of a paycheck does not mean you are not responsible for many of the same items that an employer might have deducted for you.

This is where I will stress again how valuable having a good accountant is. Even though you see 100% of the revenue your business generates does not mean you should spend it all. You will have to pay income taxes personally, and possibly on the business as well. There are also those payments that are due for Social

Security as well as a self-employment tax that the IRS assesses. Sometimes these payments are due quarterly, others annually, but due all the same. Your ignorance of this fact will not hold any clout when they do finally catch up to you and the amount owed by that point could be very high. In these instances the IRS can garnish your future wages, put a levy (a freeze) on your bank accounts so that you can no longer access your own money and possibly go so far as to throw you in jail. From a banking standpoint, they are allowed to freeze double the amount you owe to account for any associated legal fees. Any of these events can turn a flourishing business into a distant memory.

Sales tax is another important aspect of being self-employed that many people overlook, and laws vary from state to state and city to city. But in most places the sales of certain goods and services are taxable. For example, in New York City all purchases, with the exception of groceries and clothing under $110 per item, are subject to a sales tax of 8.875%. That's why that $5 menu item at McDonald's actually ends up costing you $5.44, to account for the sales tax. Many first time entrants into the business world of sales and service do not realize they are responsible for charging their customers this extra amount, setting it aside and then filing a quarterly return with the state where all of these transactions are listed and ultimately paid for. Sure, you can try and hide the fact that you made these sales but if you accept a credit card as payment or are filing an income tax return the state will find out eventually. And when they do the possible penalties are the same as not paying income taxes.

Student Loans

This section was kept intentionally separate from other kinds of debt that you may incur over the course of your life, the kinds that can have a negative connotation like credit card debt, but also where you typically are receiving something tangible in return. What makes student loans so fascinating is that, depending on where you go to school and the field you choose to study, you can spend more money than on a mortgage in some parts of the country – all the while with nothing "tangible" to show for it. Unless of course, you view that piece of paper called a diploma as tangible. This is not a knock on education at all, simply a perspective that many people oftentimes overlook when it comes to how and where we spend our money and incur our debt. Colleges can be the best investment or the biggest waste of money ever, all depending how you approach it.

College is not for everyone; that should be of no surprise. Nothing in life is for everyone. If we were all meant to play the piano music would inherently lose some of its appeal. The same goes for education. If everyone decided they needed to go to school to become architects and engineers there would be no one around with the physical skills to actually build their creations. This is a philosophy that was lost on me when I was younger as no one ever asked what I wanted to do when I grew up, or what I was interested in. Instead, the only advice I got came from two opposing camps in my family. One was the "go to college and get a good job" argument. The other was the "get a civil service job like a cop or a fireman and retire in twenty years" rebuttal.

I went with the first option and wound up with a degree I don't want in a field I hate. Oh, and a boatload of student loan debt I was not even aware I was incurring – coming back to that in a minute. Looking back on option two that I became convinced was beneath me at the time, my twenty years of service would be up this year and had I made that choice I would be retiring at the age of thirty-eight with a pension coming in every month and the freedom to do what I really want without concern for money – write.

Okay, enough about me. Let's get back to those student loans. There is a fine line between grants that do not need to be repaid and student loans that do. From the federal government, they go by all kinds of crazy acronyms like Pell, FAFSA, and TAP. There are also private student loans, but those tend to be a little more obvious on what you are getting yourself into. When you are about to graduate high school and go to college, or if you happen to be a parent of someone about to embark on that journey, *financial aid* applications are slid under your nose one after another to the point where your hand will hurt from signing them all. To be clear, aid does not mean free. Because it is for educational purposes, many of these federal student loans have relaxed credit standards or history requirements, or none at all. Some parents can take out solely in their own name, others they must cosign for the student.

The co-signing for you part is where the trouble can begin. Once you graduate from college or stop going for whatever reason, those loans will become due and someone is going to have to start making payments every month. That can be a shock to the system as an unemployed nineteen to twenty-year-old. It can be as much or more of a shock to the parent of that young person who unwittingly signed their name, because when payments are not made, both parties – parent and child – will wind up with negative credit reporting. Sometimes the loan companies will work with you if you call up and ask for deference or reduced payment options but that is far from a guarantee. They may even tell you the only way to avoid making payments is by remaining a student.

Now don't laugh. Millennials are the most educated generation in history. I have known people who were perpetual students. Not because they had a thirst for knowledge, but because it delayed the inevitable task of becoming an adult. As long as they remained in school they did not have to repay any of the loans, didn't have to move out of their parents' basement, give them a dime for rent or look for a job. But eventually, everyone winds up having to face reality. You can either do it with your eyes wide open and have a plan for how to tackle those bills when you get out of school, hopefully by getting a job in the field you studied, or you can blindly graduate with four degrees in unrelated subjects and no viable job options along with hundreds of thousands of dollars in student loan debt.

Back to that decision about whether or not to go to college now that you have some insight as to the responsibility involved. There are certain professions where it is an absolute requirement, such as a doctor or lawyer. Those also happen to be the jobs where the more prestigious your college and sizable the student loan debt, the higher you are likely to be paid after graduating. There are some other fields along those lines as well, like engineering or nuclear physics, but I leave the research portion to you. The point I want to bring out is, unless you were absolutely positive about what you want to do after college there is no need to rush into accepting NYU's offer to spend $50,000 dollars on a philosophy degree (actual tuition figures based on the 2016-2017 data).

Not many people will tell you with brutal honesty that your first two years of college are not that important. I don't mean that from a goofing off standpoint, but from one that focuses on where you choose to go. In your Freshman and Sophomore years, the majority of the classes you will be taking are considered to be the school's "core curriculum" so you may find your schedule loaded with English, Math, Science, even Philosophy classes when they have nothing to do with what you will ultimately major in. You do not have to declare your major until entering your Junior year of college, and this is where the rubber meets the road so to speak –

most of your coursework will revolve around that particular major and the associated field it falls in. So if you major in Finance, there will be numerous classes in the different areas of finance plus other aspects of business such as accounting and statistics.

Knowing this, there is no reason to spend $50,000 or more on a private college or Ivy League school for the first two years if you are not absolutely certain of what you want to do. Even *thinking* you have an idea of what to do should give you pause to commit as you enter the college environment and get exposed to new thoughts and concepts. There are plenty of community colleges, city and state universities where you can earn an Associate's Degree (2 years of study) and then transfer to a college of your choosing afterward that specializes in what you have decided to major in.

There is one word of caution to this method though, and that is around the transferability of credits. Just because you get your Associate's Degree does not mean that the school you want to go to will accept all of the credits earned from that two-year school. Sometimes losing a few credits is not the worst thing in the world considering how much money you saved, but be sure to meet with someone in the Admissions Department to discuss what will and will not transfer over. If it looks like too much money will be lost, take the time to research some other schools that specialize in your intended major and consult their admissions staff as well.

So can you survive in life without going to college?

Absolutely. To my earlier point, there are plenty of opportunities out there that do not require any college. There are skilled trades such as plumbers, electricians, and carpenters who can make great money – especially if they are fortunate enough to get into a union. Some type of vocational school or apprenticeship may be required in order to obtain your certification or license but these are generally far cheaper than college, can be paid for by your company or union, and will be much more enjoyable if it is something you love. Police and firefighters are other occupations that do not require anything beyond a GED to start. As you climb the ranks it may become advantageous to differentiate yourself from others who are also looking for promotions by taking some college coursework, but you can earn a decent salary complete with full medical benefits and a pension without incurring any student loan debt.

Retirement Accounts

If you thought the Rule of 72 was powerful, there is another concept that actually *compounds* just how effective it can be – tax-deferred or tax-free growth of your money. As a rule of thumb, all interest you earn in your everyday savings and investment accounts, so long as it is over $10, is subject to taxation. That can really put a damper on your long-term earnings, especially as you make more money and they take more money.

But thankfully the IRS does allow for a way to avoid paying

taxes on the interest you earn. Of course, it's not always the most helpful to you today. When stashing money away for your retirement you have the option of putting a special designation on those funds – IRA, which stands for Individual Retirement Account. There are 2 different types of IRAs that we will cover, but the underlying principles and rationale for both are the same. There was a time in this country when almost all companies or employers offered pension plans to their employees, where a worker didn't have to do anything more than work there in order to receive money at retirement each month for the rest of their lives. Because of a large portion of the American workforce not having any incentive or plan to prepare for retirement on their own, the IRS decided to make it more appealing for us to save money by offering tax advantages.

The first option is a Traditional IRA, simply called such because it was the original plan devised in 1974. With this option, if you are under fifty years old the IRS will allow you to contribute a maximum of $6,000 per year from your earned income, so yes you must have a job "on the books" in order to take advantage of it. Two things happen from this point on that can shift your financial well-being. The first is that you are now allowed to deduct whatever amount you contributed from your income for the year. If you put in the maximum of $6,000, then your annual income will reflect as 6,000 less – an amount you don't pay tax on. Secondly, all of the money inside your Traditional IRA grows tax-deferred until you withdraw it, which allows your money to work harder for you. It is important to note here, though, that you should not touch this money until the age of at least 59½. Should you decide to withdraw anything before that it will be subject to not only a 10% penalty from the IRS, but will also get added to your taxable income for the year and incur further deductions.

The other option is more of a newcomer, having only been established in 1997, but a very popular one so long as you make under a certain dollar amount every year, and that is the Roth IRA. The contribution limits are the same as the Traditional IRA, but the rest of the mechanics are slightly different. There is no tax deduction of your contributions each year, but that is partly attributed to the fact that all earnings grow completely tax-free – that's right, even when you hit 59½ there will be no tax on those withdrawals. The Roth also allows you to withdraw any interest earned, so everything but your contributions, without incurring that 10% penalty and hit to your current year's tax situation.

There are important things to note about the use and regulation of IRAs:

➢ The maximum contribution limit of $6,000 is a combined total for both Traditional and Roth IRAs. So if you choose to have and contribute to both, which is perfectly acceptable so long as you meet the requirements, you will have to decide how to split that $6,000 dollars between both accounts.

➤   It is always advisable to consult with an accountant before starting either of these plans if you are unsure which would be the best for you.

➤   IRA is not a type of account, it is merely a label to the IRS that gets plastered on any one of the types of savings and investment vehicles we spoke about in Banking 101. So your IRA funds can be held within a savings account, CD, or any range of investment options. Do yourself a favor and don't just walk into a bank and ask to open an IRA, have some prior thought put into it so you appear knowledgeable enough not to get sold on whatever products they happen to be pushing that day.

Matthew Harms

Future Planning Worksheet:

1) Identify three areas where you might have an interest or ability in starting your own business (baking, jewelry making, etc):

2) If you have not yet gone to college, search the average tuition at the top three schools of your choice:

3) Research what the average salary (using glassdoor or payscale) for each of the proposed professions you want to go to school for and see how long it would take to repay the tuition if you were to use 100% of your salary to repay the loans:

     (A) Estimated Annual Salary

     (B) Estimated Total Tuition

     (B/A) Years to Repay Loans

4) Identify three places that you would like to open an IRA with, then decide on one or a combination of the three along with how much money you can put away monthly:

     -Company   -$$$$

"The world is full of obvious things which nobody by any chance ever observes."

-Arthur Conan Doyle

Chapter 10: The Not-So-Obvious Stuff

"Common sense is not so common." Have you ever heard that expression before? I'm not sure if I encounter it more often than I say it, or vice versa, but either way it holds incredible insight into our society. There are so many things in life we either take for granted or accept at face value that it is downright scary. We live in an age of media and news coverage overload with a constant barrage of information that is represented as factual. Too many of us believe everything we are told. Sometimes, that is because we want it to be the case. Other times, it is because it takes less thought and effort on our part to go against the norm.

I can't lie and just say that I have been an outsider looking in on some of these things that scream of improbability, the lure of life being simple and fair is an easy one to fall victim to. But you live and you learn. One of the things that I tell the students I work with these days is to *question everything!* You cannot lose anything by looking for more information. Knowledge is, after all, power. Do not feel embarrassed or ashamed to ask a friend, coworker or expert in a particular field about something that you are unsure of. Even if you think you are sure but it is an area where you have no experience or understanding, seek out advice, coaching or guidance before going any further.

Voting

This is a tricky topic even for this book. Since I try to stick to topics that I never learned in school this was not one that immediately jumped out at me. But as I got to thinking more about it, even in talking to many of the people I went to school with, it became clear that not every school teaches the mechanics of voting and those who have heard it before often have different interpretations of how it works. It's voting, how complicated could it be? Think about the science of breathing, an activity that comes naturally but involves so much more than meets the eye. Before you even decide to register to vote, there is a decision you might want to give some thought.

There are many elections where you must first align yourself with a political party before you will be allowed to vote. There are two main parties who control all of the politics in the United States – the Democrats and Republicans – but the mechanics behind that is a conversation for another book entirely. You can also choose to register as an Independent if you find nothing particularly appealing about the main parties. This gets a little confusing because you can still vote in many elections even if you have not registered with a political party.

The elections you will not be allowed to vote in are the ones known as "primaries." These are the elections where each party, almost always Republicans and Democrats, is narrowing down which candidate they are going to have run in the "general election" against the other party's candidate. In order to vote in a Democratic Primary you must be a registered Democrat, and vice versa for the Republicans. With that said, it is important to be registered to vote as soon as you turn eighteen so you have the ability to vote in any city, state, or national election and you can do so at www.usa.gov/register-to-vote.

Voting is not something that should be taken lightly. Politics in this country is very complicated along with a few other not so flattering adjectives that will be left unsaid. The act of voting should never just consist of going out on Election Day and pulling an arbitrary arm for a candidate because you like their face, someone told you to do so, or because they belong to a specific party. As a registered voter you have one of the greatest freedoms in the world, something that people kill and are killed for in many other countries. But with great power comes great responsibility. Our elected officials, especially city and state level, have a tremendous impact on our everyday life and in picking someone without fully understanding what they stand for and how their policies can impact you, the point of voting becomes diluted and meaningless. We live in an age of information and the amount of resources at our fingertips allows us to thoroughly investigate each candidate without having to rely on what they want you to believe through the one-sided campaign advertisements they run.

This brings me to my next point. Do not accept anything at face value in life – that goes double when it comes to politics.

Grow Up!

Politicians are in positions of power and that power becomes something that many are not willing to cede easily and will go to great lengths to maintain. Much like researching a candidate before you vote for them, the same should apply to picking a party allegiance. America happens to be an abnormality in the world of democracies by only offering people two parties to choose from and it can become very easy to get bogged down in the "us versus them" mentality those parties spew against each other. The worst thing you can do is pick a party solely because that is what your parents happen to be or because your community pushes you in that direction. People are psychologically resistant to change which has created part of the inertia in the two-party system. Use your judgment and see which side, if either, actually speaks to you before committing. If it is neither, and that's perfectly all right, then register as Independent or don't pick a party at all. Maybe one day you will be able to help change the system, but the only way to accomplish that is to vote in the first place.

Throwing this last part out here strictly because I recently learned something new that changed the way I think about the presidential election process, and I like to believe I am not the only one who had this belief. When we vote for president we are actually not voting directly for the candidate, but instead for the Electoral College who then turns around and casts votes for the president. That means there is a chance that more people could vote for one particular candidate and they still lose the election because the other candidate got more electoral votes. That was supposed to be theoretically impossible by design but has actually wound up happening in two of the last five elections. So if you voted with the majority and lost it can be easy to feel like the system is broken – again a topic for a whole other book – and that your vote was pointless. And while that is true in terms of the election itself, polling data can be analyzed later to add insight to certain trends. For example, if one million popular votes were cast for the losing candidate, and a large percentage of those million voters identified as Independent or having no party affiliation, it could go a long way to show just how many people out there have given up on both major parties and possibly spark the change that I mentioned earlier.

Scams of Life

These are so common today that I have decided to go back and add this section to the book. Everywhere you look it seems like someone is trying to separate you from your hard-earned money. And unfortunately, the people who engage in this kind of activity are very, very good at what they do and will lose no sleep if you fall victim to their scam. To some of you, a lot of what I am about to say may sound like common sense and you have no idea why it's here, but almost all of us at one point or another have wanted some of these things to be true.

Lottery scams are huge. Here is how it works. You will get a call or a letter from someone, usually based overseas, to tell you that you've won the lottery. Sometimes there is a limited amount of time for you to claim the winnings (so that you don't have an opportunity to consult with anyone who may talk you out of it) and in order to do so you must first pay the taxes on the winnings, and it must be done as a wire transfer. The obvious part that makes this a scam is the request for upfront payment of taxes because as you now know taxes are paid at the end of the year. In legitimate lottery winnings, your estimated taxes will be withheld from the payout check you receive. The next part is that you probably have never visited the country in question, much less played the lottery there, so how did you win? The wire transfer part seals the deal because those are guaranteed funds and in almost all circumstances cannot be reversed or disputed after you uncover the fraud. I have literally stopped dozens of people from sending wires like this during my career in banking.

Next, are the responses you may get to items you listed for sale online or jobs you applied for. Craigslist is a notorious breeding ground for these types of scams but they can happen anywhere and for any item. The way it works is that someone responds to your listing and offers to pay you more than what you are asking, usually to cover shipping or some other special service they are requesting. They will then send you a check and ask you to send them back the extra money you did not use. To be clear, the point of this scam is not to get the merchandise. If they do, great. But what they really want is for you to deposit the fraudulent check and send back the cash. Shortly after, your bank will deduct the check from your balance once they realize it was fraudulent, your account will get frozen and the con artists just got free money. That is also how the employment scams work as well, although in those instances they will tell you the check is to purchase the equipment you need to work from home and send them back the balance.

The next two scams tend to target the elderly more but they are important to be aware of. Scammers will call and say that they are the IRS and that you are going to be arrested for not paying taxes. Sometimes they won't say IRS, just that if you don't send a certain amount of money you will be taken into custody. Neither the IRS nor any other government or legal agency will ever call you to warn of such a thing. They will either send you an official letter, have someone personally serve you legal paperwork, or simply send the police to actually arrest you. The other phone scam is saying that a friend or loved one has been hurt or arrested and you need to send money right away. Needless to say, don't do it. If you think it might be true, contact the person in question first to put your mind at ease.

There are probably a few more that escape me at the moment but the bottom line is that there is no way to get something for nothing in life. If it sounds too good to be true it probably is. Scammers prey on our greed and emotions in order to further their own agendas and the more they get away with it the more they will try. Oftentimes they will tell you not to mention it to anyone and the red flag should be obvious but if not, always do your research. Check with someone at your bank, Google the company or contact information for who you are supposedly dealing with, or look up the check online if you went that far and see if the routing numbers and remitter information match. Usually you will find numerous posts from people stating that the same folks scammed them. Last time I checked no one was handing out free money, and that's not likely to change any time soon.

Cocky vs. Confident

There is a common theme amongst many of the youngsters I work with that I find hard to explain. That is a sense of entitlement that oftentimes borders on delusion. The world does not owe anyone anything – period! To think otherwise is just setting yourself up for failure.

Let's start with delusion. Nothing is given out for free in life, at least for the most part. I hear so many of the kids I teach tell me they are going to be a professional athlete when they grow up so they don't need to learn reading and writing. While the second part of that statement is not true under any circumstances – the quickest way to have folks like agents, managers and financial advisers steal all of your hard-earned contract money is to be uneducated and allow it to happen, the first part should not be dismissed outright. I do truly believe that any person has the opportunity to be or do anything they want in life.

Yes, a minuscule percentage of kids who play a sport in grammar school ever go on to play professionally, most not even making it to the college level arena. But some do. Heck, these days it has proven that anyone can truly even become President of the United States. The fault I find with that statement is when I follow up to support them and ask how often they practice. The answers almost always range from: in gym class, in the park after school, or on the weekends. I hardly ever hear that they play eight hours a day, take two hundred jump shots a day, or kick a soccer ball wherever they go. No one is born great. Born with talent – yes. But that talent needs to be honed and refined. Show me one professional athlete who got where they are as a gym class hero.

Next comes entitlement, which is way worse than delusion because there is a more active choice being made. Just because you can be anything you want doesn't mean you deserve it more than someone who worked just as hard, if not harder than you did. I am going to pick on education and employment for a moment and hopefully that alone is enough to prove the point. So many young people today feel they are above working a certain kind of job because of the stigma associated with that type of work, or because they feel they are too educated. A good work ethic and willingness to learn and do difficult tasks will go further than any education ever will. *"I went to (insert school name here). I have this advanced degree and that kind of specialized training. That job should have been mine.* Have you ever heard any of those statements before?

Reminder: Millennials have been, in general, classified as the most educated generation in the history of America. Do you know what other dubious distinction they also hold? They are also the most unemployed by percentage of all age groups. If you are having difficulty connecting the dots let me give you a hand. Millennials are competing with a pool of people who are just as qualified as the person next to them! Guess who gets employed first? Generally, the one who is willing to start with a less prestigious position or pay grade in order to prove their worth. In other words – someone less entitled.

Work ethic is not something that can be taught in school. And luckily it's not a talent like singing or drawing that you have to be fortunate enough to be born with. This is a trait that you develop and foster over time. The best way to do that is by putting 110% effort into everything you do, even if it is less than appealing or you feel it is beneath you. CEO's are not born – they are made. And in many instances they have worked their way up from the mailroom to the boardroom. If you are sitting around waiting for that Fortune 500 Company to call with an Executive level position solely because of your education, you better get a comfortable chair because it will probably be a while.

<u>Not So Obvious Worksheet:</u>

1) Decide if you want to join a political party after doing your research:

     -Republican

     -Democrat

     -Independent

     -No party

2) Register to vote!

3) List five adjectives that describe yourself in a confident way instead of cocky:

4)List five accomplishments you are most proud of that could be highlighted in a positive way to advance your career or image in the eyes of an employer:

Closing Thoughts

Life is not about the destination; it is the journey that counts. Along the way, there are going to be countless situations and events that arise in which you will have to make a choice, possibly a series of choices. There is nothing wrong with making mistakes or choosing what turns out to be the wrong path in that instance. The key is to be open-minded and receptive to learning from each experience. Sometimes the best lessons are learned from not succeeding on your first attempt at something. One of my favorite quotes on the best way to approach failure is from Michael Jordan.

"I've missed more than 9,000 shots in my career. I've lost almost 300 games. 26 times I've been trusted to take the game winning shot and missed. I've failed over and over and over again in my life. And that is why I succeed!"

Coming from one of the greatest basketball players to ever live, that statement is huge. Our mistakes do not define us, but how we react to them can. There is also something to be said for learning from the mistakes of others as well. No two people have the same path in life, but the wisest among us know that we can grow through the experiences of those who came before us. There is no silver bullet or magic wand for everything life throws at you, but we do live in an amazing era where we have access to so many tools that can help us make the most informed decisions possible. It would have been impossible to cover everything in this book, but hopefully the topics that were presented will help set you up for success and guide your thinking process when confronted with a difficult choice. You can follow me at www.penforhirenyc.com for updates and new work.

In closing, I would like to give a special thank you to a few people who have really gone above and beyond to help me with this project:

➤ Doreen Geiger-Leeds for her invaluable input from a Consumer Advocate standpoint.

➤ John Conn for taking the time out of his busy schedule to provide the photography for the book cover.

➤ Joselito Rosario for putting the entire concept together.

➤ Heléne Rhodin-Shillingford for all of her coaching and support in the marketing and design of both "Grow Up" and the newly revised "Employed!"

➤ Last, and certainly not least, thank you to my son and mini-me, Jax, for being so cooperative in serving as the muse and focal point for the cover. Cash, you get the next one!

Appendix:

1-1: Amortization Table of a 200k mortgage over 30 years with

balances owed at the end of each year.

Year	Principal	Interest	Total Paid	Balance
2019	$1,211.59	$4,156.61	$5,368.20	$198,788.41
2020	$3,012.66	$9,871.02	$12,883.68	$195,775.75
2021	$3,166.80	$9,716.88	$12,883.68	$192,608.95
2022	$3,328.83	$9,554.85	$12,883.68	$189,280.12
2023	$3,499.13	$9,384.55	$12,883.68	$185,780.99
2024	$3,678.15	$9,205.53	$12,883.68	$182,102.84
2025	$3,866.34	$9,017.34	$12,883.68	$178,236.50
2026	$4,064.15	$8,819.53	$12,883.68	$174,172.35
2027	$4,272.08	$8,611.60	$12,883.68	$169,900.27
2028	$4,490.66	$8,393.02	$12,883.68	$165,409.61
2029	$4,720.40	$8,163.28	$12,883.68	$160,689.21
2030	$4,961.91	$7,921.77	$12,883.68	$155,727.30
2031	$5,215.77	$7,667.91	$12,883.68	$150,511.53
2032	$5,482.63	$7,401.05	$12,883.68	$145,028.90
2033	$5,763.10	$7,120.58	$12,883.68	$139,265.80
2034	$6,057.98	$6,825.70	$12,883.68	$133,207.82
2035	$6,367.92	$6,515.76	$12,883.68	$126,839.90

2036	$6,693.69	$6,189.99	$12,883.68	$120,146.21
2037	$7,036.16	$5,847.52	$12,883.68	$113,110.05
2038	$7,396.15	$5,487.53	$12,883.68	$105,713.90
2039	$7,774.55	$5,109.13	$12,883.68	$97,939.35
2040	$8,172.31	$4,711.37	$12,883.68	$89,767.04
2041	$8,590.40	$4,293.28	$12,883.68	$81,176.64
2042	$9,029.92	$3,853.76	$12,883.68	$72,146.72
2043	$9,491.92	$3,391.76	$12,883.68	$62,654.80
2044	$9,977.54	$2,906.14	$12,883.68	$52,677.26
2045	$10,488.01	$2,395.67	$12,883.68	$42,189.25
2046	$11,024.58	$1,859.10	$12,883.68	$31,164.67
2047	$11,588.63	$1,295.05	$12,883.68	$19,576.04
2048	$12,181.51	$702.17	$12,883.68	$7,394.53
2049	$7,394.53	$123.79	$7,518.32	$0.00
Totals	$200,000.00	$186,513.24	$386,513.24	

1-2: Amortization Table of a 200k mortgage over 15 years with balances owed at the end of each year.

Year	Principal	Interest	Total Paid	Balance
2019	$3,011.79	$3,314.57	$6,326.36	$196,988.21
2020	$9,341.86	$9,637.22	$18,979.08	$187,646.35
2021	$9,819.76	$9,159.32	$18,979.08	$177,826.59
2022	$10,322.18	$8,656.90	$18,979.08	$167,504.41
2023	$10,850.26	$8,128.82	$18,979.08	$156,654.15
2024	$11,405.38	$7,573.70	$18,979.08	$145,248.77
2025	$11,988.91	$6,990.17	$18,979.08	$133,259.86
2026	$12,602.28	$6,376.80	$18,979.08	$120,657.58

2027	$13,247.03	$5,732.05	$18,979.08	$107,410.55
2028	$13,924.79	$5,054.29	$18,979.08	$93,485.76
2029	$14,637.21	$4,341.87	$18,979.08	$78,848.55
2030	$15,386.07	$3,593.01	$18,979.08	$63,462.48
2031	$16,173.25	$2,805.83	$18,979.08	$47,289.23
2032	$17,000.70	$1,978.38	$18,979.08	$30,288.53
2033	$17,870.49	$1,108.59	$18,979.08	$12,418.04
2034	$12,418.04	$233.96	$12,652.00	$0.00
Totals	$200,000.00	$84,685.48	$284,685.48	

1-3: Calculators representing the normal payment amount and additional principal payment of $25 per month on a 30-year mortgage:

With No Acceleration	
Estimated Monthly Mortgage Payment (Principal and Interest) ($)	$1,074
Number of Required Monthly Mortgage Payments	360
Total Interest Expense over the Mortgage Term ($)	$186,510

With Acceleration	
Amount of Overpayment ($)	$25
Total Estimated Monthly Mortgage Payment Paid by Borrower (Principal, Interest and Overpayment) ($)	$1,099
Number of Required Monthly Mortgage Payments with Acceleration	341
Reduction in Number of Monthly Mortgage Payments	19
Total Interest Expense over the Term of the Mortgage with Acceleration ($)	$174,734
Reduction in Total Interest Expense over	$11,776

1-4: Calculator representing the additional principal payment of $85 per month on a 30-year mortgage:

With Acceleration	
Amount of Overpayment ($)	$85
Total Estimated Monthly Mortgage Payment Paid by Borrower (Principal, Interest and Overpayment) ($)	ⓘ $1,159
Number of Required Monthly Mortgage Payments with Acceleration	ⓘ 305
Reduction in Number of Monthly Mortgage Payments	ⓘ 55
Total Interest Expense over the Term of the Mortgage with Acceleration ($)	ⓘ $153,410
Reduction in Total Interest Expense over the Term of the	ⓘ $33,100

1-5: States requiring real estate attorneys present at closings (current as of August 2019):

Alabama, Connecticut, Delaware, District of Columbia, Florida, Georgia, Kansas, Kentucky, Maine, Maryland, Massachusetts, Mississippi, New Hampshire, New Jersey, New York, North Dakota, Pennsylvania, Rhode Island, South Carolina, Vermont, Virginia, and West Virginia.

7-1: Sample Medical Plan Overview:

Important Questions	Answers	Why this Matters:
What is the premium?	**$481** monthly	The premium is the amount paid for health insurance. This is only an estimate based on information you've provided. After the insurer reviews your application, your actual premium may be higher or your application may be denied.
What is the overall deductible?	**$2,500** person / **$7,500** family Doesn't apply to preventive care	You must pay all the costs up to the deductible amount before this health insurance plan begins to pay for covered services you use. Check your policy to see when the deductible starts over (usually, but not always, January 1st). See the chart starting on page 2 for how much you pay for covered services after you meet the deductible.
Are there other deductibles **for specific services?**	Yes; **$300** for pharmacy expenses	You must pay all of the costs for these services up to the specific deductible amount before this plan begins to pay for these services.
Is there an out-of-pocket limit **on my expenses?**	Yes. **$2,500** person / **$7,500** family	The out-of-pocket limit is the most you could pay during a policy period for your share of the cost of covered services. This limit helps you plan for health care expenses.
What is not included in the out-of-pocket limit?	Co-payments, premium, balance-billed charges, prescription drugs, and health care this plan doesn't cover.	Even though you pay these expenses, they don't count toward the out-of-pocket limit. So, a longer list of expenses means you have less coverage.
Is there an overall annual limit **on what the insurer pays?**	No.	The chart starting on page 2 describes any limits on what the insurer will pay for specific covered services, such as office visits.
Does this plan use a network **of providers?**	Yes. See www.insurancecompany.com for a list of participating doctors and hospitals.	If you use an in-network doctor or other health care provider, this plan will pay some or all of the costs of covered services. Plans use the term in-network, preferred, or participating for providers in their network.
Do I need a referral to see a specialist?	No. You don't need a referral to see a specialist	You can see the specialist you choose without permission from this plan.
Are there services this plan doesn't cover?	Yes.	Some of the services this plan doesn't cover are listed in the "Excluded Services & Other Covered Services" section.

Questions: Call 1-800-XXX-XXXX or visit us at www.insurancecompany.com.
If you aren't clear about any of the terms used in this form, see the Glossary at www.insuranceterms.gov.   1 of (

Matthew Harms

Common Medical Event	Services You May Need	Your cost if you use a		Limitations & Exceptions
		Participating Provider	Non-Participating Provider	
If you visit a health care provider's office or clinic	Primary care visit to treat an injury or illness	$35 co-pay/visit	40% co-insurance	—none—
	Specialist visit	$50 co-pay/visit	40% co-insurance	—none—
	Other practitioner office visit	20% co-insurance for chiropractor and acupuncture	40% co-insurance for chiropractor and acupuncture	—none—
	Preventive care/screening/immunization	$0	40% co-insurance	
If you have a test	Diagnostic test (x-ray, blood work)	0% co-insurance	40% co-insurance	—none—
	Imaging (CT/PET scans, MRIs)	0% co-insurance	40% co-insurance	—none—
If you need drugs to treat your illness or condition More information about drug coverage is at www.insurancecompany.com/prescriptions	Generic drugs	$10 co-pay (retail); $10 co-pay (mail order)	40% co-insurance	Covers up to a 30-day supply (retail prescription); 31-90 day supply (mail order prescription)
	Preferred brand drugs	20% co-insurance (retail and mail order)	40% co-insurance	—none—
	Non-preferred brand drugs	40% co-insurance (retail and mail order)	60% co-insurance	—none—
	Specialty drugs (e.g., chemotherapy)	0% co-insurance		—none—

Questions: Call 1-800-XXX-XXXX or visit us at www.insurancecompany.com.
If you aren't clear about any of the terms used in this form, see the Glossary at www.insuranceterms.gov.

Common Medical Event	Services You May Need	Your cost if you use a		Limitations & Exceptions
		Participating Provider	Non-Participating Provider	
If you have outpatient surgery	Facility fee (e.g., ambulatory surgery center)	0% co-insurance	40% co-insurance	—none—
	Physician/surgeon fees	0% co-insurance	40% co-insurance	—none—
If you need immediate medical attention	Emergency room services	0% co-insurance	40% co-insurance	—none—
	Emergency medical transportation	0% co-insurance	40% co-insurance	—none—
	Urgent care	0% co-insurance	40% co-insurance	—none—
If you have a hospital stay	Facility fee (e.g., hospital room)	0% co-insurance	40% co-insurance	—none—
	Physician/surgeon fee	0% co-insurance	40% co-insurance	—none—
If you have mental health, behavioral health, or substance abuse needs	Mental/Behavioral health outpatient services	0% co-insurance	40% co-insurance	After 8 visits, not covered.
	Mental/Behavioral health inpatient services	0% co-insurance	40% co-insurance	—none—
	Substance use disorder outpatient services	0% co-insurance	40% co-insurance	—none—
	Substance use disorder inpatient services	0% co-insurance	40% co-insurance	—none—
If you become pregnant	Prenatal and postnatal care	Not Covered	Not Covered	—none—
	Delivery and all inpatient services	Not Covered	Not Covered	—none—
If you have a recovery or other special health need	Home health care	0% co-insurance	40% co-insurance	—none—
	Rehabilitation services	0% co-insurance	40% co-insurance	—none—
	Habilitation services	0% co-insurance	40% co-insurance	—none—
	Skilled nursing care	0% co-insurance	40% co-insurance	—none—
	Durable medical equipment	0% co-insurance	40% co-insurance	—none—
	Hospital service	0% co-insurance	40% co-insurance	—none—
If your child needs dental or eye care	Eye exam	Not Covered	Not Covered	—none—
	Glasses	Not Covered	Not Covered	—none—
	Dental check-up	Not Covered	Not Covered	—none—